HOW TO GET TO HEAVEN
WITHOUT GOING TO CHURCH

How to
Get to
Heaven
Without
Going to
Church

William Aulenbach M.Div., M.S.W.

Creative Ventures
P.O. Box 33
Dana Point, California 92629
1-800-305-8240, 714-240-2933, Fax 714-489-3773

Printed in the United States of America.

Editing: PeopleSpeak
Book design: Joel Friedlander Publishing Services

In Appreciation of

THE EPISCOPAL ACADEMY, a college preparatory school located in the suburbs of Philadelphia, where I first learned the thinking process.

KENYON COLLEGE, a liberal arts college in Gambier, Ohio, whose professors sophisticated my thinking process and taught me how to question the world around me.

THE CHURCH DIVINITY SCHOOL OF THE PACIFIC, an Episcopal seminary in Berkeley, California, whose professors helped me change my Sunday School theology into a practical Christology that can be used on a daily basis.

ANNE, my wonderful, beautiful wife, who has loved me, supported me, and helped me develop a theology that even works at home.

A CHRIST who *really* makes sense.

Contents

Introduction

IT WAS EARLY EVENING and the telephone rang. "Hi, Father Bil, this is Sally Martin. Do you have a minute?"

"Yes, Sally. It's good to hear your voice again."

We chatted about what was happening in her life, the new baby, and her mom and dad. (I had married Sally and her husband a few years earlier; we had stayed in touch on a casual basis.)

"I have a feeling that you called me about something more."

"Well," said Sally, "it has to do with our daughter. She's almost a year old and some friends are putting pressure on us to have her baptized. They kind of imply that she'll go to hell if we don't get her baptized. Is that really true?

"I was baptized—Catholic—but I never really went to church. It was so boring. My husband wasn't baptized. He's sort of willing, but he doesn't believe in hell. He's been in a recovery program for many years and does talk about his relationship with a Higher Power; it's very important to him. A couple of times a week he goes to his meetings. Never misses. But he's not so sure that he wants to become involved in a church. He says, from his point of view, churches appear to do a lot of arguing among themselves. He sees them like a big business—sort of like McDonald's with a franchise on every corner.

1

"Neither of us is really sure what it means to be a Christian. There appear to be lots of different 'brands' of it: they have different rules, they differ over what the Bible says, they try to make you feel guilty about not being perfect, they try to force you to believe their way. Look at the abortion thing. It's awful. They talk about love and the importance of life then they go around and beat up people who don't think their way. They destroy buildings. Is that what Christian love is? Christians will tell you that they love everyone—but not if you're gay or divorced or have an abortion. Then they don't love you but call you names and tell you you're going to hell. Sorry, Father Bil, I've rambled on, but I'm really confused. Do we need to have our daughter baptized?"

I told Sally that she'd asked a lot of questions. "I wouldn't want you to have your daughter baptized until you have answers to your questions. Tell you what I'm going to do. I'm going to write a book that will answer your questions." We both sort of laughed.

"I'll get to work on it right away. Be patient. It will probably take me a week or so," I said sarcastically but truthfully.

Then I suggested that she, her husband, and I get together and really discuss the issue of baptism and what it might mean to the three of them. We set a date.

After we hung up my mind started racing. Sally had asked a lot of hard questions, but I have heard these questions and reactions to the church and Christianity many, many times. Sometimes I feel like a broken record trying to justify Christianity and church to others.

For a period of my ministry, I took on the role of "the defender and apologist" to those who were critical or questioning about either subject. Then I stopped because I found that the conversation ended when I felt the need to defend. In retrospect, I discovered that what many were questioning was correct. After all, it was the way *they* saw it. One of the questions they asked most frequently is, Why do Christians seem to fight among themselves so much?

Is that how we appear? We *do* do a lot of arguing in our own denominations. We also do it with other denominations—considering that there are over five hundred "brands" or "schisms" of Christianity. About the only common denominator we have is that we all use the name Jesus. But there does not seem to be much similarity concerning who he was/is, what he said or did, and what his primary mission really was.

Want to see a "religious" fight start? Try throwing out any of the following words: abortion, gay, women priests/bishops, lesbian clergy/ministers, sex outside of marriage, birth control, infallibility of the Bible, or ordained gays. These are all fighting words. Everyone appears to feel that *they* know how Jesus felt about each of these issues.

Wouldn't it be great, instead, to start an argument among the denominations as to who can give the most money and services to our suffering fellow humans? Most would agree that this is a role or calling for *every* Christian.

How does one become a Christian? There seem to be as many answers as there are schisms. Most use the same word: baptism. But the rules about that rite vary from simply saying "I believe" to highly ritualistic ceremonies done in large bodies of water with someone saying some magic words. Some say that if you don't do it their way then you haven't had it done—and off to hell you'll go if you don't buy into their party line.

Who gets to go to heaven? That depends with whom you speak. Some say "the predestined." Others talk about "the elected" or "the chosen." One group has a very specific number: 144,000 get to go to heaven, and that's it. Can you imagine the infighting in that group?

Who makes the final choice? The immediate response is St. Peter at the Pearly Gate. He will have his big list of pluses and minuses. He will go down that list, right in front of us, perhaps humiliate us or make us feel awful. Then the *big* decision: stay or go south for eternity! Is that really going to be the way? I don't know about you, but if that is the case, I don't have much of a chance. This brings up the next question.

What about all of my good works? Don't they count? Going to church, saying prayers, reading the Bible regularly, eating fish on Fridays, giving a peso to a beggar, not flipping off that obnoxious driver on the freeway. They *must* count for something. But how do I know? Who will tell me? My mother? My minister? My conscience? How am I going to find out?

The questions appear endless. The more questions one asks, the more there seem to be.

The number of askers are almost as endless. It seems that every time I go to a function and talk with people about this book, they want to order a copy on the spot. People are hungry for the Gospel—the Good News—to be in touch with a Higher Power, but they are confused. They try to ask questions but only get a narrow answer. Somehow or another they start feeling guilty and sometimes dumb if the other person starts quoting Scriptures. Very soon the other person starts to push them to join and all they wanted to do was ask a question.

Christianity has become so complex and complicated that I am not so sure that any Christian knows what Christianity *really* is today. At times, when Christianity is discussed on television or in the newspaper or I see the way people act as Christians, I too become confused. Then I have to ask myself my standard questions: "Is this really what Jesus wanted?" "Did he really hang on the Cross for this?"

Sometimes I have a great deal of difficulty correlating what goes on in the name of Christianity today with the actions of a poor Jewish peasant from a small farming village who had little formal education but a great deal of charisma and a very strong message to *love*.

I suspect that there are other people who might have some of the same feelings. Many of them are looking for a christ (or a savior or messiah) but see Christianity as so complex that they stop looking to the institutional church for help. Thus this book was written to help Sally, her husband, and others gain some insight into what basic Christianity really is and how it can help us in our daily living.

For me, the whole premise of Christianity is based on the idea that those who believe that Jesus is the Christ are saved by their faith—and their faith alone. *Absolutely nothing else is needed.* That sounds really easy. Maybe for some it sounds too easy because some place in the back of our heads a little axiom comes forth: "There is no such thing as a free lunch." Salvation should not be easy. It has to be earned with a lot of blood, sweat, and tears.

But the honest truth is that salvation is ours for the asking. That's the Gospel. In this book, I will show you, Sally, and her husband not only how simple it is to become a Christian but also how exciting it can be to live as a Christian on a daily basis. Christianity gives good answers to the possibility of life after this one. It helps us to deal creatively with guilt. Christianity can teach us how to deal with the curve balls that keep coming our way.

Our journey will be a reasonably simple one and progress naturally—sort of like building a house. First, we are going to lay the foundation (chapter 1) and keep building until we complete our structure—a solid house ready to move into and enjoy to the fullest (chapter 12).

The first chapter talks about life as it really is. Some might see it as pessimistic or a little negative, but *realistic* is the key word here. Think of life as a rose garden with some beautiful flowers but with plenty of thorns.

In chapter 2, I want to introduce you to a man for whom I have a great deal of admiration. I am sure that you have heard about him, but do you know much about his humanity? Most people don't. We shall look at his life from the viewpoint of four books in the New Testament and do a little speculation about some of the things he did. We will look at his death and what happened after that in a later chapter.

Chapters 3 and 4 present God and the Holy Spirit in a unique way. An understanding of who they are and how they function might be much easier than some think, especially as these ideas fit into the progression. In chapter 5, we are going to tackle the subject of evil and the Devil. Even though many try to ignore the power of this force at work, we can't. We need to recognize this power and deal with it creatively.

Chapter 6 contains some thoughts about the Bible that will allow us to develop an understanding of its place and importance in our lives. It is a source of great information but can also be a source of misinformation and confusion. We need to be very clear about its importance in our journey.

The seventh chapter looks at death (daily and final) and starts to prepare us for chapter 8, the Good News, which is the heart of the faith and this book. It's a "how to": how to put all of this into action in our daily living so that we can meet the challenges (thorns) with renewed hope and courage. It is because of these actions that our lives will make unbelievable changes based primarily on one day in the short life of one man who was legally murdered some two thousand years ago.

In chapter 9 we shall learn the law of love and atonement; chapter 10 is about prayer. The eleventh chapter looks at the role of the church in the Church. Then we tie the whole thing together so that we can move on creatively with our lives as well as be able to

1. discern when the Good News can be bad news,

2. make the Good News work for us on a daily basis, and

3. deal creatively with the bad news.

Look up "heaven" in a dictionary and you'll find references to a wide variety of definitions and interpretations. Consider

- the abode of God

- the angels, and the spirits of the righteous after death

- the place or state of existence of the blessed after the mortal life.

In speaking with others (theologians and regular churchgoers), you might hear definitions such as "the place where the redeemed will receive their eternal reward." Some consider heaven as the visible sky while others write about the place having angelic and demonic powers. It is obvious that heaven means many things to many people on many different levels.

When I use the word "heaven" I am not referring to a place (up there or anywhere) but rather a feeling of being "at one" with myself, my fellow human beings, and my Creator. I don't feel that the church (or any church) is going to give me the ticket to get to heaven (no matter how that term is defined). I do believe that the key is to center my life on love and take my marching orders from my Christ, who tells me and shows me how to love.

I have never known what gender to call God. Part of the reason I wrote this book is to worm out from under this dilemma. Occasionally, I do use the word God, but to then use "he/she" or "she/he" makes for boring reading. So every time you see a "he" or a "she" after God just pretend I wrote "he/she" or "she/he." Reread my last two sentences and I think you'll see how monotonous this could be throughout an entire book.

If you are interested in reading more of the Bible citations mentioned here, please be aware that all biblical quotes can be found in the Revised Standard Version.

So when you are finished with this book, you will know and understand exactly how I believe you, your loved ones, or anyone can get to heaven without going to church. While one vision of heaven (somewhere "up there"—a gossamer cloud with harp-playing angels) is a very pretty picture, it's not my picture. Heaven is ours when we can each find a peace within ourselves by loving and accepting ourselves as fallible but creative humans.

Let's head off to the jungle.

CHAPTER I

Living in the Jungle

HAVE YOU EVER HEARD the expression "Life is a jungle"?

In Hawaii in the 1960s, there was an area behind beautiful, luscious Waikiki with its high-rise buildings and picturesque beach and surf known as "the jungle." It was dreadful. Here lived the drug addicts, prostitutes, homeless, helpless, poor, and every example of humanity at its lowest. The area was badly run down, and no one seemed to care very much as long as the people who lived there stayed there. As a part of my work with youth, every year I would take a small group of teenagers from a private school on a neighboring island and go live in the jungle. For five days they would experience what life was like there. It was a real eye-opener for this group of middle- to upper-class youth. They never realized that jungles exist in every large city and that in each jungle one will see people in all sorts of conditions.

Jungles are relative. We all live in one to some degree. Maybe it's our home, marriage, friends, family, neighbors, neighborhood, our work, the freeway, or the inner city. Some people live in a jungle full time, some only part time, and others for a few moments as they drive through. Jungles are a part of life.

Have you ever been in a real jungle? The Marine Corps put me in a few, and if you have not been in one, let me describe the experience.

As we approached a jungle, we had no idea what was in there: foliage, animals, people, or danger. We saw the density but didn't really "feel" the jungle until we entered it. Then we often encountered bushes, vines, and trees so thick that a human being couldn't even see through the growth much less walk through it. The machetes came out and the hacking began. Sometimes clearing a path would go on for hours.

Fear—some real, some imagined—was a standard feeling in the jungle along with a miserable sensation of being trapped. Usually, there was but one path and not a lot of room to operate from it. Our fantasies often went wild as we continued to hack away at the brush. We knew that the enemy could be only a few feet away, well camouflaged, and ready to blow us to bits. Jungles were (and still are) a constant challenge.

Jungles were often melting hot and chest-crunching humid. With sweat pouring down us, we also would start thinking about the animals that might be out there: snakes, lions, wild boars, bears, poisonous insects, etc. It was an uncomfortable, out of control feeling, and we had no idea what would happen next. At times the jungle was very noisy; at other times the silence was deafening. Suddenly, an animal would bellow or a noisy bird would start screaming above, and our hearts raced to our throats.

Finally, we would hack through the brush to a clearing—only to have to pick up our machetes again twenty feet down the path. On and on it would go, often for days at a time. Jungle life was tough.

Over the years, I have felt that a great similarity exists between daily living and what takes place in a jungle.

1. We all have our *fears*. Some are big, some not so big. Some are real, some imagined; but they are there.

2. Life offers *constant challenges*. In one way or another, almost on a daily basis, we seem to be hacking through some sort of obstacle. Challenges never seem to stop coming.

3. We also have feelings of being *trapped*. Our job, marriage, responsibilities, children, taxes, credit cards—anything can entrap us.

4. Finally, we face the *control* issue. Who or what is running our lives? Who is in charge? Am I? Or is it some other force?

Let's look more closely at these four characteristics of the jungle in light of our own lives.

First, a little exercise. Take a moment and think about your life and the jungle issues in which you are involved. What are the issues? Write them down as you see them. (Please use pencil here and elsewhere unless you want others reading your answers.)

_____

_____

_____

_____

_____

Now let's look at some of the issues that all of us deal with on a continuing basis. Let's start with our fears.

FEARS

Every human being has fears. Some people suppress them so much that they don't even know that they have them, or at least they won't admit it.

I suspect that the most prevalent fear for many human beings is that of death. How painful is it going to be? What is going to happen when this old body stops functioning? Do I just become "ashes"? Is there anything on the other side of death? God? St. Peter? Angels? Satan? Fire? Pain? We fear death so much that most people make no preparation for it because they really don't want to talk about it or deal with it. Do you fear death?_____

Another universal fear is that of being unneeded or unwanted—that no one cares or will care when we are old and decrepit. Maybe the children are grown and the nest is empty and lonely. So much of our early lives was centered around them, but now they are involved in their own thing. Perhaps our significant other has left us, or maybe she is so involved in her own activities that she doesn't have time anymore. Maybe we have retired from the work that was our life. Do you feel unneeded or unwanted?_____

Closely aligned with this is the fear of being unemployed—we won't be able to find another job. We could lose our home, our car(s), our possessions. Above all, we could lose our dignity, our identity—maybe even become one of the legions of the homeless. Homelessness knows no social or economic boundaries. I have been in that unemployment line. It was good for my humility, but it felt like hell on earth. I can remember vividly those feelings of being unemployable, useless, washed up, a disgrace. After the tenth "Sorry, we are not going to hire you," it became almost unbearable. Have you ever been in this position?_____

Speaking of rejection, it's another great fear of humanity. We are afraid that no one will like us. Perhaps we have a handicap—real or imagined—and we see ourselves as unloveable. It appears no one wants to be around us. They won't hire me, marry me, date me, talk to me, even be nice to me. Do you ever suffer from the fear of rejection?_____

How about the fear of losing our health? On an annual basis, I seem to go through the routine of "falling apart." Every ailment I ever had comes back to haunt me. That sore neck from a skiing accident kicks in, my lower back aches, the pad of my foot needs another shot of steroids because it's so painful, an old ulcer hurts, and on and on. Is it a tumor? Brain cancer? Heart disease? Stomach cancer? How long do I have to live? Will my death be fast and easy or long and hard? Sound familiar? Do you ever fear for your health?_____

Another common fear is abandonment. Perhaps you were abandoned as a child and the fear has spilled over into your adult life. Perhaps a parent, or both parents, walked out and you are still in pain. You vowed not to let it happen again, but now you are in a terrible relationship. There is no love, no caring—only indifference, hurtful behavior, anger, and/or cruel words. But you hang in there because you can't stand the feeling of being abandoned. (Think of how scared you would be alone in the jungle!) Does this sound familiar?_____

What fears of yours have we not touched on? Take a moment and write them down.

_____

_____

_____

_____

_____

_____

The next jungle trait we want to examine is that of constant challenges.

CONSTANT CHALLENGES

We think that we are finished hacking our way through one clump of impenetrable brush, and then around the next corner stands a new clump. My mother thought that when she was older and retired, many of life's "clumps" would go away. On her death bed, at the age of ninety-one, she said to me, "Bil, life is troubles!" In other words, the challenges *never* stop coming.

One challenge that *never* stops is decision making. Every day, in so many ways, we are faced with having to make decisions. Some are really easy: tea or coffee, shower or bath, local or national news on television. Others aren't quite so easy: whether to find a new job, go to a new school, or join a new church; buy a new car, dress, or toy; or go to Europe or Hawaii on vacation. Some decisions are very difficult: move far away, go into bankruptcy, get a divorce, call the police about my child, seek help for an addiction. Almost every decision has positives and negatives, and some can have devastating consequences. Some people hate to make decisions for fear that their choices will be "wrong." Others make decisions but then don't want to live with the results. Is decision making difficult for you?_____

Our next challenge is conflict. It's around us almost as much as decision making. Some people attract it; they appear to be in constant conflict with someone, whether at home or work, on the freeway, in a store, or wherever they are. Then at the other end of the spectrum there are those who never seem to be in conflict—primarily because they will avoid it at any cost. They will let everyone walk all over them trying to pretend that it does not matter. But inside it does, and many of these people have tremendous internal conflict. In the middle there are the rest of us who encounter conflict almost on an ongoing basis. It could be from our significant other, children, parents, boss, or colleagues or from people at school, in stores, or on the freeway. We try to pretend that it doesn't bother us, but within our deepest self it is very upsetting. Is conflict (or lack of it) an issue in your life?_____

Closely aligned with conflict are the clashes that exist between parents and children. They start when the children are about two years of age and continue rather steadily until about age twenty-five. Then, for the most part, everyone is so tired of the confrontations that they stop or at least slow down. Remember trying to get your children ready to go to school, church, or an appointment in the morning? The time is usually from 7:00 A.M. to 8:00 A.M. and is referred to by some as the "arsenic hour." It's one of the times that we get "sickness unto death" of our children. Someone once said, "If (at times) your children don't make you sick, you have sick children!" Ever been sick of your children?_____ Or parents?_____

Let's look at another constant challenge: criticism. We love to give it (usually under the guise of being "constructive"), but most of us sure don't like to be on the receiving end. Even though we often pretend that it doesn't hurt, deep down it does. As we are giving criticism, we seldom think of how painful it has been when receiving criticism. We forget how insulted we were or how hurt we felt as the attack engulfed us—but we continue to point out weakness(es) in other people. Are you a critical person?_____ (If you are not certain, ask your significant other, a fellow employee, or a neighbor.) When criticized, do you become hurt or insulted easily?_____

Anxiety presents another constant challenge. Anxiety differs from fear, which is an emotion based on reality. Fangs showing, the snarling pit bull running right at us is real! Fear sets in immediately. However, anxiety is an emotion based on a false threat. We see the pit bull lying unleashed in the front yard; our mind sees that pit bull charging. This is anxiety. After all, the pit bull hasn't even moved. Some of us become anxious about things that have not yet happened. Others are anxious all of the time about anything and everything. Are you an anxious person?_____

Last on my list of constant challenges is "peace of mind." We seem to be constantly looking for the answer as to where we can find this peace. Look at all the peace-of-mind articles and books available. Some people even develop anxiety over not finding this peace.

Be honest. Is there really any such thing? Maybe for a few minutes, but then life will present another challenge. Are you constantly seeking peace of mind?_____

Now it's your turn. Write down your constant challenges if they weren't already mentioned above.

Now back to the jungle and the idea of being trapped.

TRAPPED

Many people feel trapped by life. Some people are trapped but are so numb that they don't feel it. Do any of these obvious things that trap us pertain to you? Alcohol?_____ Drugs?_____ Tobacco?_____ A lousy job?_____ A bad marriage?_____

An affair?_____ Loneliness?_____ Anxiety?_____ A sick relationship?_____ An obsessive/compulsive habit?_____

Hate also ensnares with less obvious traps. We hate someone, something, or some group so badly that our lives go out of control when we encounter it or them. Hate can kill—us and them. But there seems to be something in many of us that just loves to hate. Remember how we used to sell war bonds (World War I and II) based on our hatred of Germans and Japanese? Then after the war, we could hardly sell a bond based on the love of our country. Has hate trapped you?_____

How about guilt? A cloud of guilt surrounds many. They feel guilty about almost everything. Guilt rules their lives. Almost every human feels guilty about something. One time a bishop asked in a sermon, "How would you like the worse thing that ever happened in your life to be printed on the front page of tomorrow's newspaper?" Does that make you cringe? What does it do for your guilt? Are you trapped by your guilt?_____

Others are trapped by a dreariness of life. Living is boring, uneventful, and not much fun. For some, even a vacation can be dreary. You go away and overeat, overindulge, and oversleep. Every year you go to the same place and do the same dreary thing. Is life dreary for you?_____

There are others who feel trapped by a feeling of restlessness. Nothing seems to work; life isn't progressing. Everything seems to be going downhill. Nobody is happy where they are!" Are you happy where you are?_____

Where else do you feel trapped?

_____

_____

_____

_____

_____

_____

Our final jungle characteristic or feeling is being out of control.

OUT OF CONTROL

Who or what is controlling your life? Is it you or some other person or force such as A parent(s)?_____ A child(ren)?_____

A drug?_____   Work?_____

Anger?_____   An "ex"?_____

A "sicko"?_____   Guilt?_____

Hatred?_____   A childhood incident?_____

Suppressed feelings?_____

You name it:

_____

_____

_____

_____

_____

Let's try some others. How about "people monsters"? These are people who knowingly or unknowingly have you wrapped around their little finger—and you put up with their "garbage." They treat you like dirt, and you go back for more. Is there anyone like that in your life?_____

Jealousy also can be an "out-of-control" issue. It can rear its ugly head at work, in relationships, at home, or with a neighbor (who just won the lottery). We are jealous creatures, especially when a person gets a promotion at the office (and we thought that we deserved it) or friends go off on a long romantic trip, inherit a fortune, or marry the person of their dreams. Are you a jealous person?_____

How about self-pity? Poor me! A friend of mine claims that he is going to write a book entitled "Self-Pity—Six People Out of Every Half-Dozen Have It." We think that no one has troubles like we do. Are you wallowing in self-pity?_____

Let's talk about organization and disorganization. People can be out of control on both ends of the spectrum. Take the average desk. Some highly organized businesspeople have two desks—one for work and one for show. Ever notice the president's desk? He has nothing on it. Does that mean he has nothing to do? I am not sure of the answer to that, but I suspect that he has another desk piled high with things to do. It's been said, "People with messy desks are creative." My wife—and her desk—are very creative. But too much—or too little—in terms of any area can easily be seen as a control issue. Are you out of control with your organization?_____ Or disorganization?_____

How else are you out of control? Take some time now and make some notes.

_____

_____

_____

_____

_____

Let's stop and take inventory here. Get a pencil with a good eraser. Now go back to the beginning of the chapter, and if you have not already done so, put a very light check mark in the blank spaces that are relevant. Be honest because no one else is going to see it. Now go back and count your checks. There are a minimum of 44 possible spaces, and there could be more depending on some of the jungle issues you might have added. What was your total?_____ Now check it against our "Jungle Meter."

- 30 to 44 spaces checked: This book could be very helpful!
- 10 to 30 spaces checked: Welcome to the club. Keep reading. There is hope ahead.
- 4 to 10 spaces checked: Please call me. I am looking for a co-author to help write my next book about peace of mind.
- 1 to 4 spaces checked: Please send me $99.95 for one of our special "Canonization Kits." When you return it, we shall name a special "Saint's Day" in your honor.
- 0 spaces checked: You should write a book. You're perfect.

Discouraged? Don't be. We are all in the same boat—perhaps just in different seats. We have painted a picture of the jungle that might be disturbing, but we are not going to walk away from it. Thus our next question, and perhaps the most important: "Who will give me the strength to meet the challenges of 'the jungle'?"

I think I know that someone. But before I introduce you to that person, let's review some basic premises about our humanity. Get your pencil. How do you feel about the following statements?

1. Every human being is unique and special. No two people are alike.

   Agree?_____ Disagree?_____ Not sure?_____

2. God does not create "junk"!

   Agree?_____ Disagree?_____ Not sure?_____

3. Every human being has a special gift(s)—something at which they are more skillful than others.

   Agree?_____ Disagree?_____ Not sure?_____ (Some people's special gift, because of lack of self-esteem, is their belief that they have nothing, let alone a special gift. Satan loves these folks.)

4. As insignificant as we might seem, each human being is extremely important in the big picture of Creation.
   Agree?_____ Disagree?_____ Not sure?_____

5. Every human being has a role to play in keeping Creation creating.

   Agree?_____ Disagree?_____ Not sure?_____

6. We are born free to pick and choose, to make decisions.

   Agree?_____ Disagree?_____ Not sure?_____

7. Each of us is in charge of our own life.

   Agree?_____ Disagree?_____ Not sure?_____

8. Each of us is responsible for what we do in our own life.

   Agree?_____ Disagree?_____ Not sure?_____

9. Some day we shall have to face what we have done with our lives.

   Agree?_____ Disagree?_____ Not sure?_____

10. Every human being is looking for a christ (a saver, savior, rescuer).

    Agree?_____ Disagree?_____ Not sure?_____

I agree with all of the above ten statements. How about you?

Are we at all close? At this stage we don't have to be. For now we just need to agree to disagree.

Remember, if you want to share this book, don't forget to go back and erase all those little marks. Your jungle inventory is no one's business but your own.

For information Leading to the Apprehension of

JESUS OF NAZARETH

Alias: Christ, Lord, Master, Rabbi, Son of God, Son of Man, Light of the World

Wanted For: Sedition, criminal anarchy, vagrancy, and conspiring to overthrow the established government

Description: Dresses poorly. Said to be a carpenter by trade. Is ill-nourished. Has visionary ideas.

Associates with common working people, the unemployed, and bums.

Alien—believed to be a Jew.

Professional agitator.

Red beard, marks on hands and feet the result of injuries inflicted by an angry mob led by respectable citizens and legal authorities.

REWARD

Now I want you to meet my friend who in less than one day revolutionized the world.

CHAPTER 2

Jesus,
The Human?

*There are three main religious groups in America.
They are called Catholics, Protestants, and Jews. How
are these three groups alike? They all worship God.
How are they different? The Catholics and Protestants
believe in a Savior. His name is Jesus Christ.*

*The Jews do not believe that Christ is their Savior.
Who do they believe Christ is? They believe he is a nice
Jewish boy who went into his father's business. So
much for our first lesson in religion.*

EVERYONE HAS A CHRIST. The word is not the surname of
a man who lived two thousand years ago. In those days there
were no family names. Jesus was known as Jesus of Nazareth,
bar (a Hebrew word meaning son of) Joseph and Mary. The
word "christ" is a descriptive word. It comes from the
Hebrew word meaning anointed, or the anointed one, the
messiah, savior.

Everyone is looking for a savior. I think we have all tried
lots of them. Think of all the saviors you have tried.

For some, their savior is alcohol. It's in a bottle and it works—until the next morning. Or drugs—great until the money runs out or the law runs in. For others, their savior is their work. They believe in the Protestant work ethic.

Then there are those who think their possessions—their things and money—are going to save them. As a teenager, I thought that by having a car I would be the most popular young man on the east coast. It really didn't work that way. I got my car, but I still was a fat boy with pimples.

Perhaps your savior is your psychotherapist or your minister, who will lead you to the "Promised Land." If it's a therapist, you are willing to pay him or her a hundred dollars plus per hour to save you. If it's a minister, you are willing to pay nothing because "It's his job!"

Some of us believe that other people are our saviors, until we discover that they are just as messed up as we are. There are some people who look to their biorhythms, the stars, or their horoscopes on a daily basis and believe that these are their saviors.

Who or what is your savior(s)?

_____

_____

_____

Check all that apply (use a light pencil with a big eraser).

_____ money	_____ body	_____ books
_____ pro sport(s)	_____ drug(s)	_____ TV
_____ movies	_____ church	_____ car
_____ house	_____ parents	_____ fishing
_____ golf	_____ booze	_____ sex
_____ job	_____ children	_____ Santa Claus
_____ children	_____ significant other	
_____ the president		

The big question always is, Does *anybody* have a savior who/that really does the job of saving? Christians believe they do. His name is Jesus. He is not a Christian—never was.

There are many misconceptions about who this man Jesus was and is. People are constantly taking away his humanity. Over and over, people say that he is divine. But the church, at the Council of Nicea in 325 A.D., worked hard at establishing the fact that "the life of Jesus is completely and fully a human life."

Some people don't want Jesus to be human. He just looks like one and acts like one—but he's really God. The nails through his hands didn't hurt and the horrible agonizing pain of the Cross was just play-acting. Many people are afraid that if Jesus had been a human, he would know how we act and feel good *and* bad—and that is threatening. (It also knocks Jesus off the pedestal some put him on.)

Personally, I love Jesus' humanity. Without it, he wouldn't—or couldn't—be my christ.

People want to make Jesus a Mr. Milk-Toast: noncontroversial, nonconflicting—just a sweet, lovely man who loved everyone. Perhaps those people have never read the twenty-third chapter of Matthew. Jesus attacked the religious leaders by saying "sweet" things such as, "They do all their deeds to be seen by men. . . ." "They love the place of honor at feasts and the best seats in the synagogue. . . ." "Woe to you, O Scribes and Pharisees, hypocrites, because you shut the kingdom of heaven against men. . . ." "You blind fools!" "You blind guides, straining at a gnat, and swallowing a camel!" "You cleanse the outside of the cup and the plate, but inside they are full of extortion and rapacity (covetous). . . ." "You are like whitewashed tombs which outwardly appear beautiful, but within are full of dead men's bones and all uncleanness. . . ."

This was just Jesus warming up when talking about the religious leaders of his day. At times, Jesus could be meaner than a junkyard dog: the way he snapped at Peter, put down the poor gentile lady who just wanted to be saved, and asked not-nice questions.

Do you envision Jesus as asexual? The movie *Jesus Christ Superstar* shocked people when it suggested, very surreptitiously, that perhaps Jesus did sleep with Mary of Magdala. Personally, I want Jesus to be a sensual, sexual person who had to deal with the same sexuality problems as you and I do. And it would be okay with me if Jesus were a homosexual or bisexual because in no way does *his* sexual preference make any difference as far as his powerful message to us is concerned.

Or do you believe your Jesus is a first-century Houdini— an incredible magician? His bag of tricks was fantastic: walking on water, raising dead people, walking through closed doors. For some, that's why Jesus is the Christ—he could do magic! Jesus would still be my christ if he had done *no* magic or tricks or miracles.

A few people see Jesus as the first president of the Temperance Union—he never had a drink and was so against liquor he served grape juice at the Last Supper. His twin brother made all that wine at the wedding party in Cana of Galilee. Quite frankly, my fantasy says that what Jesus really made at that wedding party was a smooth '26 Chardonnay with a marvelous fruity bouquet.

I think most people see Jesus as perfect. (See Appendix A, Obscene Words and Phrases.) How one defines that depends on what one considers "perfect." Is it flawlessness? Who judges? Is it saying or doing the right thing? Who sets the standard for what's right? Was Jesus perfect? The pig farmer whose herd drowned because of the demon Jesus put in them obviously didn't think too kindly of him. The religious leaders thought he was a jerk. His family thought he was a "psychoceramic" (a crackpot). Judas Iscariot didn't have much respect for him. On and on goes the list of those who thought that he was not perfect.

Frankly, I don't need a christ who is perfect. I need one who has experienced what I described in chapter 1—someone who knows imperfection in himself as well as others. A sinless christ is a fantasy, especially if we define sin as "separation." (We will explore this further in chapter 5.) There is no way one can be completely human and sinless. Part of every human's humanity is sinning or missing the mark. Jesus missed the mark many times according to the Gospels. And he is still my christ—in spite of his human frailties.

It is important to have Jesus be "divine." Webster's defines "divine" as "supremely good, superb, Godlike." I see Jesus as divine in the sense that from a Christian's perspective he was supremely good (if you ignore how the religious leaders, the pig farmer, and Pontius Pilate felt). But sometimes, some people make him so divine that there is no way he could possibly be human. The reverse is also true: that he could be so human that he couldn't be divine.

However, I see humanity, you and me, as divine. We are creatures of Creation, and God doesn't make junk! We can be supremely good. For example, St. Paul, St. Francis of Assisi, Mother Theresa, and the countless folks who keep those philanthropic groups going all can be considered extremely good. But because of our freedom, we can also be hellishly bad. The important thing is not to make Jesus so divine that those nails in his hands and feet didn't really hurt.

The same idea goes with the title sometimes placed on Jesus:

"The Son of God." Aren't we all sons and daughters—the children—of Creation? We are part of Creation. We were born to be creative, to keep Creation creating. (I'll discuss this in more detail in chapter 3.)

Enough about misconceptions. Who was Jesus? Obviously, he was born a human being. We don't really know when this took place. In his day it was not important to remember your birthday. In the fourth century, Emperor Constantine chose December 25 to counteract a drunken holiday, but no one really knows Jesus' exact day of birth. Does it *really* make any difference?

His mother's name was Mary. A virgin? Who knows? There were no medical reports. Perhaps she was a virgin in the sense of the word's old meaning—a woman who had not yet given birth. It had nothing to do with intercourse. Mark and John found the issue so controversial that they didn't even want to tell birth stories. Matthew and Luke told two entirely different ones.

Saying nothing about a stable, Matthew tells the story of Herod and the Wise Men. He does talk about Jesus being in a house, the killing of all male children in Bethlehem, and the flight to Egypt. Luke relates the story about the birth of John the Baptist, the manger, shepherds, and an angel. These stories certainly aren't very much alike. I always like to ask those who take the Bible literally, "Now which story am I supposed to believe?" I have never received a good answer.

But what difference does it make? Suppose Joseph and Mary had intercourse. Suppose the birth stories were figments of a writer's imagination. Would that detract from the Cross and the empty tomb? Not for me. In my opinion, the Resurrection still the most powerful event in the history of mankind.

We don't know much about the childhood, adolescence, and early adulthood of Jesus. A book entitled *The Lost Books of the Bible* (Bell Publishing Company, New York, 1978) tells some wild stories about his childhood. I suspect not much of it is true.

We know that he had brothers and sisters. Matthew names them: "James and Joseph, Simon, Judas, and all his sisters" (13:55). We know that he worked in his father's carpentry shop, probably making farm implements. He didn't seem to like it very much.

Although Jesus spent much of his life getting ready, we really don't know where or how. But all of a sudden, he "appeared" and started preaching and teaching. He gathered a rather impressive group of companions in a hurry. Maybe he had known them for a long time. We have no idea how popular he really was. I suspect he was more popular than his cousin John the Baptist, who was somber and a little weird, and who had a negative message.

The ladies liked him and he liked the ladies. He had a large entourage of women who stuck by him. He also liked to party. He loved to go to people's houses and celebrate life. He had a good sense of humor, but we Westerners don't appreciate it because we don't appreciate mid-Eastern humor. For example, the imagery, the idea of a camel going through the eye of a needle, is uproarious in the Middle East. As many times as I've read that passage in church, I don't think I've ever seen anyone even smile, much less chuckle.[1]

Jesus seemed to like agitating his religious leaders. He went after them as much as possible. As mentioned previously, he was a very good name-caller. Jesus had a short fuse; he could be very snippy with his disciples and others, especially Gentiles. One could even say that he was anti-gentile.

He had some real insights into life and living, especially for a man who was really a simple peasant from a very rural background. I think he was the right man, in the right spot,

---

1. For more on this, read Elton Trueblood's fun book called *The Humor of Jesus* (San Francisco: Harper & Row, 1964).

at the right time, with the right message. What does that mean? The Jewish people were loosely enslaved by the Romans. That's humbling! They wanted to be in charge. There was a lot of infighting among them: Sadducees vs. Pharisees vs. Zealots vs. Essenes vs. the Poor vs. the Rich vs. each other. A unifying force was needed (like King David) to bring the people together to push out the Romans.

The Jews were ripe and ready for a charismatic leader like Jesus. His message was new and different. People were ready to follow him, just like others in history: Gandhi, Abraham Lincoln, Martin Luther King, Jr., just to name a few of the more recent ones.

It's unbelievable! His ministry was somewhere between one and three years old, yet he managed in that short time to revolutionize the world. He changed the course of history from B.C. to A.D. in about two years.

I am convinced that he deliberately agitated the leadership to the point of them wanting to kill him. Why? Did Jesus really want to die? Did he know that he would revolutionize the world? Did he understand and see what would happen down the road if he died? I don't know, but many presume that he knew. But how did he know? Because he was divine? Or because he was willing to risk and like so many martyrs could see that perhaps his death could bring some kind of change—at least to the Jewish people?

Whatever his reasoning, he took the risk. He pushed the religious leaders to their limit. He could have left town at any time, but he didn't. He could have gone away and let things cool down and returned later or gone to a more neutral area—but he didn't. He stayed, and he made them mad, and then madder. As a seminary professor once told me, "Jesus wasn't killed because he said, 'Consider the lilies of the field and how they grow,' but because he said, 'Consider the Pharisees and how rotten they are!'"

He died a cruel, suffering, torturous death on a cross, just like many other revolutionaries, criminals, and evil people. History reports that as many as three hundred were crucified at one time. On this day, a Friday, there were three. Jesus didn't last long on the cross—about three hours. Some people lasted as long as a week; it became a sort of power struggle. The Romans would put them up in the morning and take them down at night until they eventually were too weak and died. Not Jesus. After three hours, he quit, saying, "Father, into your hands I commit my spirit!"

Up to this point, there is really nothing unusual about what Jesus did or said. He plagiarized (the "original sin") a lot in his words and his actions. Just look at our Christian traditions. Most of them have their basis in Judaism, both as a religion and as a culture.

However, the next thing that Jesus did was and is the *only* thing that Christianity is all about: Jesus conquered death. The tomb was empty on Sunday morning. He paved the way for us to make Easters out of our Good Fridays. How do we know that he conquered death? There are no photos—no Polaroid snapshots. But there are two thousand years of history showing us that those who are looking for a workable christ can start to find one by having faith in that empty tomb, in that first Easter, in the risen Christ who can bring life out of death. The joyous occasion is the subject of chapter 8.

As Christians we are about Easter—*not* Christmas. Unfortunately, too many Christians get warm fuzzies about a baby in a manger and have little or no understanding about the empty tomb.

In this book I am going to explain the power of Easter, but first remember this: One thing, and only one thing, is really important to Christianity and to Christians. All the rest is extraneous and sometimes very confusing. The life of Jesus is relevant only when we look back on it from the empty tomb. Without that, nothing else really matters. I believe the Christian faith is based on only one thing—the empty tomb.

It's your turn. Take a few minutes to think about the question, "Who do *I* think Jesus is?" There are no right or wrong answers. Write down your ideas, not someone else's. Jesus is

_____

_____

_____

The story that is told about this picture is of a Chinese photographer, deeply troubled religiously, who took a picture of the melting snow with black earth showing through. When he developed it, he was amazed to see in it Christ's face, full of tenderness and love, and he became a Christian.

It may take you a long time to see the face, but that difficulty is perhaps a symbol of the effort that must be made to find him in our world. Once found, however, as in the picture, he dominates the scene and one wonders how it was possible to miss him.

CHAPTER 3

"Dog" Spelled Backwards = _ _ _

BACK IN THE 1960s, when God was "dead," young people would often jokingly ask this question: "What is 'd-o-g' spelled backwards?" The answer is obvious, but to some adults this was seen as irreverent. I saw it as part of some young people's reactions to negative feelings about the stereotyped picture they had about God. Perhaps they picked up these ideas from Sunday School, their parents, or misinformed preachers.

In my many years of teaching, I have heard a multiplicity of ideas about who/what God is. Whenever I taught a course, in the first session I would ask the class to share with me their ideas about God, Jesus, and the Holy Spirit. They responded with a myriad of answers, primarily because each person had had different experiences with life and with God. It's these experiences that give us our concept, our image, and our impression of God: where you were raised, what church you attended, your parents' or family's input, your friends, a divorce, and untimely death. All of these and how you live your life have helped you to discern who your God is for you.

Some examples: If you are black, I would suspect that your God is black. If you were raised in the city, your God is going to be different than if you were raised in the country. If your father was a drunken bum who beat you and your mother, sexually abused your sister, and spent most of his time behind bars, your concept of God as "Father" is going to be different from mine because my father was a loving, caring, warm human being. If you're disabled, you might envision God as a rotten s.o.b. for giving you all those handicaps. If you are a controlling human being, I suspect that your God is very controlling. If you are a vengeful person, I would think that your God wouldn't do much forgiving. For too many, God is very much like who they are with their life experiences.

Before I share some of the basic concepts I have heard over the years, let's stop a moment so you can write down some of your thoughts and ideas. Think about it for a few minutes and then jot down how you envision God.

Remember:

1. This is *not* a test.

2. There are no right or wrong answers.

3. You will not receive any celestial brownie points or demerits by doing this exercise.

4. Be totally honest because you can always erase your answer if you don't like it.

To me, God is

_____

_____

_____

_____

_____

Let's take a look at some common concepts that generally cover the different ideas people have. Our words might be different, but the general idea is going to be about the same. God is like a *Master Puppeteer*. He sits "up there." From that vantage point God can see all (even through cloud covering), hear all, and knows everything that is going on in the universe 24 hours a day, 7 days a week, 365 days a year (as if God operates on days, months, and years). One of God's biggest jobs is to keep lists (celestial brownie points versus celestial demerits). God makes *everything* happen. A good day or a bad day depends on how God feels because it trickles down to us. After all, she is pulling the strings. Does any of this sound familiar? Is part—or all—of your God a Master Puppeteer?

Our next classification is God as *Benevolent Dictator* (B.D.), who is going to run/rule the universe as he sees fit. He could be nice or maybe not so nice, depending on whether he got a cup of coffee that morning. We do not have choice(s) or any freedom. The decisions (big and little) are made "up there." Although it looks (superficially) like we are equipped to make decisions and that we are free to make choices, it's only an illusion. The B.D. makes all the decisions and usually quietly puts them into our heads, and we just follow along. If we don't do what we are told, then somehow or other we will have to pay a price. Sometimes that price can be war, hurricanes, tidal waves, volcanoes, automobile accidents, a cold, hemorrhoids, a belligerent child, a drunken spouse, you name it. All are a result of B.D.'s payback.

Let me share a story. (Honestly, I heard this one.) The Benevolent Dictator needed some children in heaven, so he picked on Susie who had had a child out of wedlock. (Shame! Shame!) To punish Susie, the B.D. gave her five-year-old daughter leukemia. After much suffering by the child and mother, the little girl died. Thus the Dictator was able to "kill two birds with one stone." (Please excuse the expression. It's about as sick as the example.) He was able to punish the mother for having had sex and then a child out of marriage as well as help fill his quota of more children in heaven. (This story always makes me ill.) Incidentally, this same kind of action on the part of the Benevolent Dictator explains why we have people who are disabled. This kind of thinking leads us into the next concept.

God is *Vengeance.* Many times in the Old Testament and a few times in the New Testament, one can get the very distinct feeling that God is very vengeful: He is going to make us pay a price for our misbehavior and our sins of omission and/or commission.

As a child, I was indoctrinated with this kind of thinking. Not in a mean or vicious way, but it stuck; and way in the back of my mind is the idea that God is vengeful. Growing up (four to seventeen years old), we lived in a two-hundred-year-old house in Philadelphia. It did a lot of creaking and groaning at night, especially when I was home alone. To get to the second floor (it had four floors) in the back part of the house, there were some steep, rickety, narrow stairs with no direct lighting. I used those stairs most of the time because my room was in the back of the house. Occasionally, I would trip going up or down. Ninety-nine percent of the time I would catch myself, but one could hear that I had tripped. If my mother was around and heard me, she would inevitably say, "Bil, what did you do wrong?" (I can still hear her voice fifty years later.)

The part that annoyed me was that she was probably right. I probably had done something wrong like not finished my homework, not completed a chore, hit my sister, called another kid an awful name, spit, cussed, told a dirty joke, or played doctor. Obviously, I was not a perfect child. So my mom was right. Even though she might not have known specifically what I had done wrong, I had done something. So God needed to punish me. One of his many ways was to make me trip up or down the stairs, and once or twice he was so angry with me that I actually fell. Oh, that God of Vengeance! I know that Mom did not believe that God was *only* vengeful, but she did believe that God would do something to you if you messed up. She was a great mom but a lousy theologian.

God is like *Santa Claus*. If you are good, then good things happen to you and you find lots of gifts under your tree. If you are bad, then you only get charcoal. One can earn celestial brownie points as well as receive celestial demerits. Unfortunately, do we know for certain what is really good, what is bad, and where to draw the line between them. Some claim to know, but do they really?

God is *Christian*. God founded Christianity in the year zero. We are not quite sure in which Christian church God has membership, but we all kind of hope that it is ours even though we suspect she is nondenominational. The irony of all this is that her son was *never* a Christian. Jesus was born a Jew and died a Jew. He had nothing to do with the start of Christianity. How did God become a Christian?

God is an *Author*. Many people say that he wrote a book called the Bible. I have heard people call it "God's Word." I am not sure what that means, and I try to ask people simple questions: What language did he use? In what year(s) was it written? How come in some parts God is so angry and vengeful, whereas in other parts God is so loving and forgiving? The only answer I ever get is that it's just "God's Word," and he can do it any way he wants.

I could go on and on giving you variations on the themes, but I think the point has been made. Every human being has a concept of God (even "There is no God"), and some ideas can be rather unhealthy. (See all of the above.) Many of the above ideas make people either so angry that they hate God or so confused that they don't really understand Christianity's big picture and continue to mouth a whole bunch of "spiritual" claptrap that doesn't make much sense. Let's move on in a more positive vein.

An admission: I believe no one (not even Jesus) knows who/what God is. My contention is that God is beyond our human comprehension. We can only describe God through our human experiences that are rather limited in relation to the universe. This is why the Bible can give such conflicting accounts of the characteristics or traits of God. The people who wrote each of the sixty-six books (or chapters or letters) were looking at life with different agendas. They experienced God with their own point of view and wrote a book about it (inspired, of course, by their God). As a result, we have about sixty-six different points of view about God in the Bible. Consequently, it is not too difficult to envision a very confusing God.

In my dealings with young people in the 1960s, I did not want to be placed in the position (because it was "no win") of having to convince youth that God wasn't dead. There was a part of me that wanted to have some of the unhealthy ideas about God be dead and buried. So I skirted the issue and said, "Okay, let your God be dead! But let me give you a new word or concept to mull around in your head. See how you like it. See if it might not be more useful." I suggested that from here on we would use another word in lieu of "God": "Creation" (which includes the words "Creator" and "Creativity"). Nothing bold or outrageous. Just another approach. This approach as to who God is stems from my experiences, which of course differ from yours. Thus, this definition is just as limited (and limiting) as any other definition from a human.

However, there are a couple of things I like about it immediately. First, it takes the image of "God looks like a human" out of the picture. Picturing God as a man with a long white beard dressed in a flowing white robe with white hair is rather limiting. God as a human implies limitations. God as Creation has no limitations. Second, we don't have to be concerned about Creation having gender, color, or creed. It's all-inclusive. It's everywhere. It's you, me, trees, dogs, the sky, the ground, and even mosquitoes. Third, we can pull away from some of those old stereotypes that can be so negative and drive people away. "Creation" is a positive word and can turn people on.

Let's look at some of the traits of Creation.

1. CREATING: Creation has created since the beginning and still continues to create the universe. It never stops. Sometimes we have a tendency to think of it as something that happened in the past. It's all told in the story of Genesis, and some folks see that as the end of creation. Genesis is a great story. The world (universe) was created in an orderly fashion, and if one changes days into millenniums, the story is identical to many scientific explanations. Certain things had to happen (e.g., air, water, land) before other things could happen (e.g., life, animals, humanity). I doubt anyone can argue with the idea that the Creator continues to creatively create. As part of Creation, we humans must do the same thing.

2. FREEDOM: There is a tremendous amount of freedom within Creation. The stars, the moon, the planets, and the Earth pretty much do their "thing" with an orderliness. We lived in Hawaii for twenty years, and I can

assure you that Kilauea Volcano on the Big Island did (and still does) its own thing.

Sometimes we have a tendency to see these acts of nature as destructive. Volcanoes kill people, eradicate communities, destroy property. We see this as destructive, but it's really Creation. Volcanoes are how Hawaii arose in the first place. Creation is the freedom to continue to create.

You and I have the same kind of freedom to creatively create or destructively destroy. And sometimes there has to be destruction before we can create (e.g., the Los Angeles riots in the spring of 1992).

As humans, we have a great deal more freedom than we think. Unfortunately, many times we either give it away or it gets taken away, and we seem powerless to do anything about it. On a daily basis, life offers us a great many choices, and we are free to pick and choose. Get out of bed or not. Go to work or not. Accomplish something at work or not. Drive the freeway or not. Drink three martinis before dinner or not. Eat too much or not. On and on. Like Adam and Eve, we have to make choices. Mess it up and it could cost us. Keep our noses clean and life will go on unless someone else makes a choice that interferes with our freedom. Then we have some new choices to make. We possess guidelines (the laws of nature as well as the laws of man) that should help us to stay out of trouble. But there is no guarantee about this. One of the strongest guidelines is the next trait of Creation.

3. LOVE: The Creator loves its Creation no matter what, even if the Creation is being destructive. Parents sometimes experience something like this with their children.

"Love" is the key word, concept, or action of Creation. It is a love that is higher than any kind of love in our human dealings; an unconditional love that loves us in spite of ourselves. It forgives instantly—if we want to be forgiven.

Interestingly, some people don't want to be forgiven. They want to wallow in their guilt and their past. These folks usually have a difficult time forgiving others.

Another key trait of this love is acceptance. Total acceptance, no strings attached. We are who we are, and that is fine with Creation. (I hope that gays, those who are disabled, prisoners, the homeless, addicts, and all of the other labeled "lepers" of our society will breathe a sigh of relief. You are loved unconditionally, regardless of what some of our "spiritual" leaders say.)

Obviously, this explanation is an oversimplification. I could spend the whole book elaborating on Creation, but that is not my objective. Right now I just want to establish Creation so that we can continue our progression. I have attempted to diffuse some of the negative, controversial aspects and present a concept that I hope can keep you moving in a positive direction.

This is the bottom line. Creation challenges me on a daily basis to be creative, loving (giving and receiving), forgiving, accepting, and always responsible for my freedom and respecting of yours. Creation can do the same for you. How? The next chapter gives some insight as we look at the source of the creative power within us.

Dog spelled backwards = Creation.

CHAPTER 4

What's This
Holy Ghost Stuff?

MANY CHRISTIANS SEEM TO BE CONFUSED by the idea
of "Holy Spirit." I wrote this chapter specifically to validate
the confusion and tell you where I find clarity about the Holy
Spirit.

For about fifteen years of my ministry I worked with
teenagers. I found that by going away to a conference center
for a weekend and dealing with youth about issues of
Christianity and the church, they gained more insight than
I could have given them in a whole year in a Sunday School
class. Although much of the weekend was devoted to no
sleep and lots of exercise (swimming, volleyball, basketball,
softball, hiking), we always scheduled "content" time—a
chance to discuss, think, and share some ideas about the
Faith.

At one conference entitled "Jesus Alive" (to counteract
the "God is Dead" movement), one young man raised his
hand and said, "Hey, Father Bil, what's this Holy Ghost
stuff?" (The church had not yet made the transition from

"Ghost" to "Spirit.") A survey of the group indicated that no one was really sure.

In my thirty years of ministry, I have seen what appears to be an almost universal confusion among the laity (and even some clergy) about the concept of the Holy Spirit. So before we go further, get your pencil (with eraser) and finish this sentence:

I think the Holy Spirit is

_____

_____

_____

_____

I have queried every study group I have ever conducted to share with me their ideas about the Holy Spirit/Holy Ghost. Over the years, I have come up with a variety of answers, but the most common one is "I *really* don't know." I find that even the church's response to who the Holy Spirit is is rather evasive. I quote from a section of the Book of Common Prayer (Episcopal and Anglican) called "The Articles of Religion." Established in the sixteenth century, Article 5 is entitled "Of the Holy Ghost," and it says: "The Holy Ghost, proceeding from the Father and the Son, is of one substance, majesty, and glory, with the Father and the Son, very and eternal God."

What does that mean? If you know, please explain it to me. Most of us don't think it says much.

So who is or what is the Holy Spirit? How does she work in our lives? Here is what I have heard people say.

- It's like a *ghost* who moves around, going through doors, telling people what to do (especially in the middle of the night). Some people confuse nightmares with the concept of the Holy Ghost: "It's scary! Awesome!"

- The Holy Spirit is like a *traffic director*: God gives a command, and the Holy Ghost carries it through. For instance, God says, "I need five new children in heaven by five o'clock Friday." The Holy Spirit then goes and makes it happen.

- Some feel this is what we get at our baptism when we receive the Holy Spirit. Baptism is going to make us "perfect" or "sinless"—from that point on. An hour, a day, a week, or a month later, we mess up and become terribly discouraged, saying to ourselves, "Here I joined the church in order to become 'perfect,' and now I've messed up again. See, it doesn't work!" And then the instant Christian becomes an instant heathen, even with the Holy Spirit in tow.

- It's my *conscience* (whatever that is—it probably should have gone on the "Obscene" list). Unfortunately, our conscience is colored by the input it receives. If the conscience has been force-fed into believing things like wives should be submissive to their husbands or (fill in the ethnicity) are inferior, then our conscience leads us to do something other than the basic Christian tenet to love ourselves, all of humanity, and Creation.

- The Holy Spirit is an "*it*." God is a he and Jesus is a he, but for some reason the Holy Ghost is an it. However, seminary professors will tell you that the Holy Spirit has to be a he because it's part of the Trinity. This man-made doctrine says that the Father, Son, and the Holy Ghost are three persons but of the same substance. They are one and the same—three different aspects of one nature.

- The Holy Spirit *guides* me. That might be okay, depending on what "guide" means. If it means that it tells us whom to marry, where to work, or how to find a parking spot at the mall the week before Christmas, then there are some problems. However, if "guide" means to be constantly aware of and respond appropriately to the Good News,[2] then I'll buy it.

I'm sure that you have even more ideas about who the Holy Ghost/Holy Spirit is and possibly have variations on these basic themes. Who is the Holy Spirit? is a good question; and we need to have a good answer because our faith cannot work at its maximum efficiency unless we do have a clear-cut understanding.

Let's go back to the idea that God is Creation and that Jesus was the most (or at least one of the most) Creative human who ever lived. The Holy Spirit follows this same line of thinking. I think the Holy Spirit is the Creation or Creativity *within* us. We are born with it, but most of the time it lies rather dormant because our destructive nature is so pervasive and persuasive. Our Creativity is often passive. Paul, in one of his letters, says it so beautifully: "For I do not do the good I want, but the evil I do not want is what I do" (Rom. 7:19). That's you and me and even bishops, presidents, and popes.

We were created to be good. (Remember: God doesn't make junk.) We also were created with the freedom to be creative. This creativity allows us to choose whatever we want, even to pick the destructive or destruction.

Many people have difficulty believing that they were created in freedom and that the Holy Spirit is that creation continued with them. These people are so controlled or con-

---

2. The term "Good News" can mean or imply numerous things. Examples include "Good News Bible"; Jesus died for us; the empty tomb; God loves us; and we are saved.

trolling they don't believe that Creation can completely abandon the control and allow them to lead their lives as they desire.

Unless one agrees with the "freedom" concept, I don't think Christianity can make much sense. If God is the hands-on director of the universe, then everything would be perfect. But we know it's not. Let me share two experiences in my own life that have forced me to look carefully at this idea of being free and using the Holy Spirit, the creativity within, to live life as I feel I need to.

The first experience goes back to October of 1958 during my second year of seminary. I had a motorcycle for good and bad reasons. Bad reason: macho image. Good reason: it helped me get around Berkeley, California, a very crowded university town with limited parking spaces. Because I was working at a couple of jobs around the city, I got a motorcycle, which could fit easily into a limited space.

On this particular day, my friend Brad and I got on our respective cycles to go to an interseminary flag football game.

Brad and I had been in the U.S. Marine Corps together. We were both captains and served with the First Marine Brigade at Kaneohe Marine Corps Air Station in Hawaii. We attended the same Episcopal church, were lay readers, and started seminary together. I was single. Brad was married to a fantastic woman. They had three children and a fourth on the way. Brad had a cycle for the same "good reason" I did. A close friend, Brad was a sensitive, loving, caring, thinking person with a great sense of humor and a real desire to share his life with others through the ministry.

It was about 3:00 P.M. on that fall Friday. I can remember us getting on our cycles. I promised to follow Brad. (He used to complain that since my bike was faster, I would leave him behind.) The next part of the story is hearsay because I have amnesia about this experience.

The story goes that as Brad and I were heading north, a fire engine answering a call was going west. It broadsided both of us. The impact knocked Brad's helmet off, and he slid along the ground until his head hit a curbstone. I went flying through the air (I wore no helmet) and landed in a garden. I was a bloody mess. The bike's handlebar brake ripped a huge chunk of skin out of my thigh, and my tibia and fibula broke the skin. At first glance, witnesses thought I was dead. When the ambulance came, they put Brad inside but immediately discovered that his brain was destroyed and he was dead. They checked me over. I was very much alive and even "chatty." Off I went to the hospital, where that night they put me back together.

I can still remember waking up in the morning wondering what had hit me. In my fuzziness, I had forgotten about Brad, but later in the morning, some friends were allowed to visit me for five minutes. I asked one of them, "Where's Brad?"

"He died."

A day or so later, a professor for the seminary came in to pray over me. He made this comment: "You and Brad must have done something terrible to deserve this." I couldn't believe my ears!

Think about this statement. I'm lying there—sore, hurting, and sad. Then this idiot with his mucked-up theology makes this stupid, insensitive remark.

I was livid. I called in some of the professors from the seminary. If that was the way God works, if this was his justice for my/our humanity, if this was his wrath, I wanted nothing—absolutely nothing—to do with that kind of God. Fortunately, the professors cooled me down, and we did a quick study on freedom.

Brad and I, of our own free choice, bought those motorcycles. (I have since renamed them "murdercycles.") Of our own free choice, we rode them on that day, at that time. I vowed to follow Brad—of my own free choice.

He could have gone flying through the air and I could have skidded along the ground. I could have been dead. He could have been alive and writing this book.

Fortunately, very early in my life as a Christian, and as a priest, I found out that I am free to direct my life, to pick and choose, as I so desire. In no way did the Benevolent Dictator do this to humble me/us, pay me/us back, murder Brad, or spare me to do bigger and better things.

Let me share one more story. Thank God my theology was in order and my connection to the Holy Spirit of creativity so strong or I'd really be angry with the Benevolent Dictator.

It was 1964. My wife and I were living in France where I was attending the University of Strasbourg and working on my doctorate. We had one child and decided we wanted another. My wife, Anne, went off of the pill and became pregnant. We were excited! But then Anne became ill. We went to a French doctor who said it was a bent uterus. Whatever it was, she was sick for a long time. We returned to the United States (the Island of Maui, Hawaii), where I was the new rector of a small parish. The baby was due in early December. Finally, on January 20, 1965, Heidi arrived. Heidi was dehydrated and weighed less than five and one-half pounds, with little red dots all over her and a mature cataract on her right eye. Six months later we discovered she was deaf. At eighteen months, after she had spent six weeks in a diagnostic center, we found out that she was slightly cerebral palsied, had a heart murmur and a mature cataract with other vision problems, and was hearing impaired; but she was *not* mentally retarded. Anne had had rubella (German measles) during the first trimester of her pregnancy, and Heidi's handicaps were by-products.

Was this the Benevolent Dictator punishing us for our sins? If so, what a cruel punishment!

Was this the wrath of God? If so, what an awful god!

Of course, it wasn't any of this.

Anne stopped taking the pill and she and I had intercourse—all of our own free choice. Everything we did, from going to France to having sex, was because *we* made decisions about where to go and what to do in our lives.

No disabled child or person is a result of a cruel decision on the part of an angry Benevolent Dictator. He or she is the result of imperfections in our universe—being imperfect but free in terms of making choices.

So many people want to control others. It's so important to tell everybody how to do everything, every step of the way. Either that or they give their own life away and allow others to control them.

Watch yourself over the next week. Observe the myriad of choices you have to make on a daily basis. See how many times you choose the Destructive, rather than the Creative. (If you have a hard time doing this, go back and review chapter 1.)

Does this mean that we can't be Creative without being baptized? Absolutely not. If one opts for baptism, it just means we are going to allow ourselves to open up to the teachings of Jesus and Christianity so that we can be even more Creative and derive that much more pleasure out of life and living.

How does all this work? It starts with each person looking for his or her christ. When we eventually get to the point of seeing that Jesus might be the answer (a christ to us), then we decide to make a commitment. And, like any good value, we must publicly affirm that commitment through baptism.

Unfortunately, the Christian church has become confused on exactly how to baptize. Arguing about the many ways, some say total immersion; others, partial immersion. A few stick your head in a bucket of water. Some sprinkle. They do it at 3 weeks of age, 12 weeks, 52 weeks, 240 weeks, 1,092 weeks. They'll do it in the ocean, a lake, the church, and a dozen other variations on this theme. I think just realizing how the church goes about setting up baptism, the various ways of doing it, and all the debate about who is right allows us to see without any doubt the power of the Destructive nature within us. It's amazing how we can take a simple act like baptism and make it into a major controversial issue of the church.

(If you promise not to tell your clergyman, I'll let you in on a little secret. Anyone can baptize anyone else. You can even baptize yourself. Now if this fact gets out, I could get into a lot of trouble, so please don't tell.)

A word about infant baptism: It never happened in the early church. The Roman emperors thought that Christians were nasty people and liked to feed them to the lions. Lions really enjoy munching on humans, and I suspect little babies are especially delicious. So what parents would be so insensitive as to make a Christian commitment for their little baby? None. Thus infant baptism wasn't even an issue in the early church. It became an issue only when some clergy saw it as a tremendous source of income and stated, prophetically, "Everyone who is not baptized is going to hell." So as soon as the lion-munching scenario ended (in the fourth century), people lined up to have their babies baptized. Thus the superstition started, and people who had not been in church since Moses died came back to the church to have this mystical power implanted in their babies to prevent their descending to hell.

Down with infant baptism. Let people make their own decisions when they're ready—not when some uncommitted, superstitious mother, father, or grandparent decides. I hope that my Creator doesn't punish a child or a baby because they haven't opted for Christianity.

At our baptism, we make a commitment that we want Jesus as "our Savior . . . obey Him as our Lord." This is the first step, the "leap of faith." The next step is to live it out. We have to learn how to make this passive Creativity work for us. That doesn't happen overnight. The Destructive is still around, working hellbent on getting us to follow its Destructive ways. Often it is fun while we're doing it. (We tend to neglect the consequences.)

We have to learn how to love—versus being indifferent or hateful. We have to learn about forgiveness—versus being vengeful. We have to learn how to love—even the unlovable; learn how to accept people as they are—in spite of their socio-economic condition, sexual preference, or skin color. We have to learn about freedom; liking versus love; reaching out and touching the hurting world; letting go of the control of others; learning and accepting how *not* to be "perfect"; getting rid of those prejudices, or at least dealing creatively with them; accepting that we are hypocrites and enjoying it; eating meat on Friday without gagging; having fun in church; having sex without guilt; figuring out who Jesus really is; reading the Bible without feeling dumb; controlling our anger; being assertive (not aggressive); differentiating between the means and the end (i.e., the church versus Jesus as Christ); and more and more and more.

What a lot of learning. It will probably take a lifetime. But it's fun to allow the Creativity within us to lead the way.

So back to our big question: What is the Holy Spirit? It's the Creation within us with the same traits—*creating, freedom, love*. Sometimes this creating is easy; sometimes it helps you to make lemonade out of lemons. Perhaps a couple of examples will make it clearer. Back to the accident on the murdercycle.

The doctors said, "It will be a minimum of an eight-week stay in the hospital." A part of me bought into that. I could wallow in self-pity, drop out of the seminary, and get that academic pressure off my back. I could mourn the death of Brad, have people feel sorry for me, and sue the driver of the fire truck and the City of Berkeley. Most of this is destructive behavior, and I don't think that it would have done much, in a positive way, for me and my life. Fortunately, Creation clicked in at this point, not only mine but a lot of other people's.

After a few days' assessment of my damages, I felt that I should spend only a week in the hospital. The doctor didn't concur, but my friends did. They cared about me, came to visit me, helped me to feel strong, important, and loved. They even brought me good-tasting food. The seminary was willing to allow me to live in a guest room next to a classroom. All my classes would meet there until I was back on my feet. They would drive me to the hospital every day so that the doctors could check me.

I could go on and on about how almost everyone's Creativity kicked in to make my life go on in a positive Creative fashion. And do you know what? In retrospect, that awful experience turned out to be one of the more Creative experiences in my life. Thank God for Creativity.

Let me finish the story about the birth of our middle daughter, Heidi. Giving birth to a child with a disability can be a very destructive event. People immediately want to know "why." Whose fault is it? The husband and wife blame each other. They fight. They get mad at the Benevolent Dictator. The grandparents become involved and start placing blame.

Divorce is often a by-product of having a child with special needs, which of course gives that child one more handicap in life. The extended family can split as a result. Guilt and shame can prevail. The family can become reclusive and embarrassed. They may not talk about it. Siblings may act the same way. They too can reject their brother or sister. One more handicap. I suspect that you see very clearly the Destruction that can go on with the birth of a child with special needs.

Fortunately, Creation and Creativity clicked in once again. We saw it as a challenge and a responsibility. First of all, we had to find out what Heidi's problems were. We had to talk about them. We had to change our priorities. I had to resign as rector of that little parish on Maui because we needed to get Heidi into a special school on Oahu. Our family learned sign language so that we could communicate with her. We had to become involved in the deaf community and find out how we could best support Heidi in her multihandicapped world.

We joined groups. We lobbied for better services. We traveled all over the country working for causes. In Hawaii we started the "Deaf Action Group" to promote the best interests of the hearing impaired. It's still going strong.

This is what I call Creativity in action. Because we are Christians, we had learned how to make Creativity happen in our lives. This has translated into every facet of our living. Now this does not mean that we can't still be Destructive in our lives. We have been, but we shall deal with that in the next chapter.

The bottom line: we used our Creativity and found we could make the positive aspects of the situation triumph over the negative. Right now, would you please be so kind as to get your trusty pencil and a piece of paper. Divide the paper in half down the middle. On the left side of the paper put the words "My Destructive Behaviors." On the right side put the words "My Creative Responses." Back to the left side. Start writing—big stuff and little stuff. Need some help getting started? How about some habits that are destructive? Smoking? Drinking? Drugs? Overeating? Sleeping too much or not enough? Watching too much television? Lack of exercise? Continuing destructive relationships? Won't talk to someone? Won't forgive? Do you hate an individual or a group? How do you treat significant others?

These are just some starters. If you are having problems remembering some of your destructive behaviors, you might review chapter 1. Be really honest because no one in the universe, not even you-know-who, is going to see that list. Then when you have enough of the left side, go to the right side and design your creative responses. Don't throw that list away. Hide it because we are going to keep coming back to write more on the left side and then design and redesign the right side.

An awesome thought: Can you imagine what might happen to this world/universe if we let our Creativity go wild? We are not quite there yet, but we are moving closer. First, however, we need to deal Creatively with the next part of our progression. What is this stuff called "evil," "sin," "the Devil," "Beelzebub"?

CHAPTER 5

"Live" Spelled Backwards =

— — — —

Why worry?

There are only two things to worry about: either you're healthy, or you're sick. If you're healthy, there's nothing to worry about. And if you're sick, there are two things to worry about: Either you'll get well, or you won't. If you get well, there is nothing to worry about. But if you don't, you'll only have two things to worry about: either you will go to heaven, or you will go to hell. If you go to heaven, you'll have nothing to worry about. And if you go to hell, you will be so busy shaking hands with all of us that you'll have no time to worry! So why worry?

DO YOU EVER WORRY or think about hell? Evil? Satan? Sin? Take a moment. Write down your ideas and thoughts about the following words:

Sin:

_____

_____

_____

_____

Satan:

_____

_____

_____

_____

Evil:

_____

_____

_____

_____

We have talked a great deal about Creation and Creativity. We have alluded to its opposite, Destruction—the Destructive Force (D.F.). It's alive, real, and all around us. It's powerful. It works very hard to win. It seems to be much more active than Creativity. For me, the very presence of the Destructive Force presents the best proof that we are born into freedom—the complete freedom to pick and to choose—to be either Creative or Destructive.

If Creation was a Benevolent Dictator or a Master Puppeteer, there would be no Destruction, and we would all be sitting in the Garden of Eden "perfect." Sin would not be a part of our humanity. Satan, the Devil, or Beelzebub would not exist, and there would be no such word as "evil." It would not mean anything. But reality tells us that Destruction exists and it looks like it's here to stay.

We call Destruction by different names: Satan or the Devil. I guess "Devil" is okay, but to me it conjures up a picture of a man in a red costume with a large mustache, evil eyes, horns, and a tail and carrying a pitchfork. He lives "down there" someplace. Like the mental image we have of God, we try to make a person or a human out of him or her.

It reminds me of the story of the two youngsters who were walking home from Sunday School after having been taught a lesson on the Devil. One little boy asked the other, "What do you think about all this devil stuff?" The other boy thoughtfully replied, "Well, you know how Santa Claus turned out. It's probably just your father."

For most folks today, this idea of Satan or the Devil looking like a man in a costume is far removed from reality. Most twentieth-century people don't buy into this image so the concept of the Devil becomes a fantasy, and with this fantasy comes the implied denial that Satan, or the Devil, or this force is real. But that's part of the force's power—to make us think it does not exist. The reality is that Satan and evil are here and working hard. It's a very powerful force and the opposite of Creation.

There appears to be confusion with the words of Destruction. We banter them about as if "Devil," "Satan," "sin," and "evil," have the same meaning. They don't. "Sin" is a very overworked word. (See Appendix A, Obscene Words and Phrases.) People try to categorize sin. Some have long lists of what sins are. Some churches also have lists of little sins, and then bigger ones, and then great big ones.

Some Christians try to pretend that they are sinless or perfect. Unfortunately, as they try harder and harder to keep up the facade of being perfect, they usually become more and more depressed and are only fooling themselves. As humans, we can't be sinless because sin is very much a part of our human condition. Some refuse to believe that Jesus said, "Those who are well have no need of a physician, but those who are sick." (Matt. 9:12) Jesus came to love the sinner (the sick). Therefore, anyone who thinks that they are sinless (or acts like it) is saying, or insinuating, "I really don't need Jesus." It's their "sinlessness" that has saved them. This really doesn't work.

In some churches, all they ever seem to talk about is sin. Everyone is a "sinner" and people should feel guilty because God doesn't like sinners. They are bad, bad, bad people. But if they drop some money in a basket, buy a book, somehow grovel in the dirt, pound their chests, or mumble "mea culpa" (I'm guilty), then they will be forgiven. We seem to have the hardest time believing that we are saved by our faith, and by our faith alone. (Actually, although theologians have always known, most people are never taught that faith alone will save them. If people knew this, clergy fear, they might never go to church.) Good works don't count as far as our being saved and having an eternal life hereafter. As Christians we must accept our limitations, our sinfulness, and work from there.

Over the years people have asked me, "What's the difference between sin and evil?" Evil is much stronger, but to really understand it one must have a clear-cut definition of sin, or separation.

From the Old Testament point of view, sin is the failure of God's Chosen (individually and collectively) to be true to the covenant with God. One could oversimplify and say the Old Testament is really the history of a four-point cycle that repeats itself over and over: (1) sin, (2) punishment, (3) repentance, and (4) deliverance. Almost every book in the Old Testament has this cyclical pattern. The New Testament breaks this pattern and eliminates punishment (from on high) and reduces repentance to simply recognizing the sin and saying "I'm sorry." Then deliverance. Unfortunately, many Christians still buy into this retributive justice (punishment) theology, and if anything awful happens (e.g., riding a murdercycle and being hit by a fire engine), it's because of some past misdoing.

Too many people get bogged down with sin and their own sinfulness. They can't move forward and allow their Creativity to work through it. As a result, I have put the word "sin" on the Obscene list and prefer to use another word, "separation."

I use another word because "sin" is such a button-pushing word, it is impossible to deal with rationally. If you say "I have sinned," some people will label you as a sinner for life—irreparable and doomed. I say down with sin! Call it separation so we can look at it calmly, discuss it, and discover what to do with it.

The New Testament is quite different from the Old. There is only one law: to love. (Remember, the Ten Commandments, the Golden Rule, and all the laws/rules your church has have nothing to do with what Jesus taught and did.) Our separation is based on not loving self, neighbor, or Creator. I believe all Christians won't be punished if one Christian separates. The New Testament puts the emphasis on the individual. He/she must take responsibility for and be in control of his/her life. He/she must be aware of his/her prideful nature and tendency to be self-centered. Each Christian must recognize each of the following realities:

- Separation is a part of our human condition.
- Every human (even the Pope) is going to separate. We have to because we as humans are imperfect.
- Now we can face facts—we don't have to pretend that we don't separate or that we are perfect.

- We can allow our separation (and all lingering guilt) to fade and die. (For more explanation, see chapter 8.)
- We musn't forget to say "I'm sorry!" or "You're forgiven!" (I explore this in chapter 9.)
- Now we are free to have our Easter. (This is discussed in chapter 8.)
- We are going to separate again. It's part of our human condition. (I originally talked about this in chapter 1.)

Let's go to a deeper level of D.F. and talk about "live" spelled backwards. Obviously, this is "evil." I am reminded of the cartoon of two young men sitting on a bench being very philosophical, and one says to the other, "If there can be no good without evil, then it stands to reason there must be a Mister Evilwrench."

Yes, Virginia, there is a Mister Evilwrench. Evil and separation are interrelated, but they are not exactly the same. One could say that all evil is separation, but only a minimal amount of separation is evil. Evil is not tornadoes, hurricanes, earthquakes, tidal waves, and so on. Those things are all part of the natural order of Creation. We tend to see them as evil because they can destroy our homes, families, possessions, and selves. Many people see or feel these acts of nature and think they are the "wrath of God." He's angry and punishing us for all our separations. And since we all separate, we buy into that easily (especially if one is an Old Testament Christian). Unfortunately, God takes the rap because nature's Creation is doing its thing—creating.

Evil is Destruction at its best (or worst), a monster with coercive force, charisma, mystery. It's not easy to define because sometimes there can be a very fine line where separation stops and evil begins. All of us have the ability to be evil. You don't believe that? How about those times when for a fleeting second you were so angry at someone (spouse, child, boss, neighbor, other driver, etc.) that you *really* wanted to kill them? Remember? Fortunately, most curbed the urge.

Or how about people in a war? For some, killing becomes fun. They become calloused to taking a human life. The evil part of them takes over. There are psychopaths and sociopaths who have no problem killing. Death row is full of them.

Very simply, one could say that "evil" is the opposite of "life." It has to do with killing—either the physical or the spirit. It's murder. Evil opposes life, liveliness, and Creation.

There is a tendency on the part of twentieth-century humanity to ignore evil. The concept seems so pagan, antiquated, unsophisticated, unscientific. This is a mistake. Evil is alive and well. It's evasive and deceptive and knows how to hide—even behind pretty faces, money, power, and prestige.

It's a very strong force that takes over some people's lives. Some individuals seem to be extremely vulnerable. They feel poorly about themselves. Perhaps they are children of alcoholics; alcoholics themselves; victims of incest, rape, or molestation; or drug addicts. Perhaps they were emotionally, verbally, or physically abused as children. Their spirits have been mortally wounded. The evil one or evil force moves in easily on these kinds of people and then starts to guide and direct their lives. As long as a person gives in (follows directions), the evil force doesn't punish them. When a person tries to resist the evil force, life can be painful—physically, mentally, and emotionally. People become suicidal and maybe even homicidal. They become abusive, can become heavily involved in drugs, or are self-destructive. Some of them have made the annals of history, but the majority of evil people live, work, and drive very close to you and me.

Right about now I can hear you saying to yourself, "This guy's crazy!" But don't throw this book away yet. Read Dr. M. Scott Peck's book *People of the Lie*.[3] He tells story after story of ordinary people who are evil.

If you asked who was the most evil person in the twentieth century, most people would probably respond "Adolf Hitler," who was responsible for the death of millions. With his gas chambers, mass executions, and torture, he tried to eliminate a whole race of people. On the other hand, he obviously was able to charm a nation into doing things his way. Many must have approved of him because he was not only able to get the power but also was able to keep it. He was able to persuade many others to do his brutal killings. He was also a vegetarian and didn't want to eat meat from animals that had been killed. This was the same man loved by the little children at his mountain retreat in Berchtesgaden because he was so friendly and warm. He loved to treat them to candy, ice cream, and cake at the same time that his henchmen were carrying out his orders to kill 6 million Jews. Hitler was evil. Satan, the Devil, Beelzebub, whatever you want to call the Destructive Force, was very much a part of Hitler's life.

Stalin and Saddam Hussein gave in to the same Force. Saddam is still giving in and will continue to do evil as long as he is around. He has sold out to evil and doesn't seem to be able to live life any other way.

Remember when the Devil tried to buy Jesus out? Jesus was vulnerable, alone in the desert, probably hungry, and fearful of what the future had to offer. He was ripe for the evil force to take over. Most of us who have been in these kinds of situations have been offered the opportunity to sell out to evil. But because of our background, environment,

---

3. M. Scott Peck, *People of the Lie: The Hope for Healing Human Evil* (New York: Simon and Schuster, 1984).

upbringing, and sense of morality, we knew how to say no and move on with our lives.

Some can't say no and give in to the Force. A mother will murder her child(ren). A serial killer will slaughter a series of young boys, prostitutes, farm laborers, or old people. Inevitably, they talk of being driven by a voice, "The Devil made me do it." The voice is real, at least to them. It must be real to us also. We can't push it aside and say that evil doesn't exist because that is when evil flourishes.

To me, there is no question that there is an evil force in this world. Destruction is powerful, and it's working in more people than we ever suspected. For me, the best way to counteract the evil force is with Creation; otherwise, evil will prevail and eventually destroy humanity, maybe even our planet. We cannot turn our backs on the Destructive Force. It's all around us, alive and well and working. At times, you and I give into the Destructive Force because it seems so much more fun (and seemingly easier) to be Destructive than to be Creative.

Our lives are full of separations. That's okay because it's part of our *humanity*.

Evil is different. It's deadly. It's not okay. We need to be aware of its presence, admit its existence, and fight it with all our might.

As Christians, we must work hard to counteract the Destructive Force. Jesus and Creation are going to teach us how. Where do we find these tools? Let's start by looking in the Bible.

CHAPTER 6

The B-I-B-L-E

WHAT DOES THE BIBLE mean to you?

Some people swear on it. Some swear by it. A few swear at it. It's the world's bestseller. Probably a large majority of people in the civilized world have a Bible in their homes. We have twelve in our house, including one in French, one in Hawaiian, and one in Greek.

One of my favorite stories is about a clergyman who came for his annual family visit. The father of the household, trying to impress the minister as to his spirituality, was telling about his daily Bible readings and devotions. Then his small son came into the room and his father said, "Son, will you please get that old book that your dad loves so well?" A few minutes later, the lad returned with the Sears catalog.

Do you ever read your Bible? How much? How often? Or do you spend more time with catalogs?

For some people, the Bible is the basis of their whole lives. They carry it everywhere. They're always reading it, quoting it, or trying to figure it out. In the 1970s, I had one such individual working for me at a camp in Hawaii. This young man read it, quoted it, and tried to jam it down everyone's throat. This was during the Watergate crisis, and that story permeated the news all day long. We heard about it ad nauseam. So one day I asked, "George, what do you think about this Watergate crisis?" He replied, "Huh? Watergate? What's that? I never heard of it." There he was with his Bible under his arm, totally oblivious to what was going on in the real world. For some reason I feel that our Creator wants us to be a part of the world—not out of it.

Some people use the Bible to escape reality. On the other hand, there are those Christians who don't pay much attention to it. Other things take priority. The Roman Catholics are guilty of this with their Missal (prayer book). For Anglicans, the Book of Common Prayer seems to be their top priority. Ask any Episcopalian to quote a Bible verse. Most can't, but many have probably memorized the whole communion service. Joseph Smith (Mormon) decided to write his own Bible. He didn't think the Christian one said it right.

Many preachers on television and in fundamentalist churches like to wave the Bible around, point at it, and quote from it.

In many homes the Bible remains unopened, unread, and very dusty. But those same people will swear *on* it that they're telling the "truth, the whole truth, and nothing but the truth." Some people see the Bible as a superstitious object, like a rabbit's foot or a horseshoe. They think there's something mystical and magical about it.

We have a lot of names for the Bible besides "Bible." It's called Scriptures, the Holy Book, the Holy Book of God, Holy Scriptures, the Word of God, the Book, the Good Book, and on and on. It's written in almost every language. For centuries the only acceptable English version seemed to be the King James edition written in 1621. It was a poor translation of the Aramaic (street Greek of Jesus' time) and often inaccurate. But no one would really say that publicly because some people thought that the Benevolent Dictator would strike you dead for such heresy.

In the 1950s, the R.S.V. (Revised Standard Version) came out. This was blasphemy, and the institutional church had a marvelous time debating it. Most of the "thees, thines, thous" were omitted. (No one without a lisp could say them anyway.) It reminds me of a cartoon in which a young person is being quoted to by her friend who says, "Once again, I quote from the Book of Proverbs. 'Who so loveth instruction loveth knowledge.'" She replies, "Yes, I loveth instruction, and I loveth knowledge." And the final caption shows her lamenting, "I also don't know what I'm thaying."

Some Christians still will not accept the new translations and continue to use the King James as if that's how Jesus and God dictated it. It's hard for them to conceive of the Old Testament written in Hebrew and the New Testament in Aramaic. To them, the King James is literally *the* "Word of God"—he sat "up there" and told people what to write. They did—word for word. Therefore, one doesn't tamper with it. One can't change a thing in it or (the subtle insinuation is) you'll be zapped dead.

Too many believe that even as intelligent human beings we have no right to question the Bible. Do you think this way?

What seems to happen is that many people get involved in the institutional church because they believe it will protect them from the real world. That means that if they do everything the church tells them to do, in the way the church wants, then they won't have any problems in the real world—the church becomes their world. As an added bonus, these individuals look at baptism like a rabbit's foot whose luck will change their lives as well.

How then was the Bible written? Like every other book—by people. People who were inspired by Creation. People who were born into freedom with all the same choices that you and I have: either to be Destructive or to be Creative. All of the Bible was written with a bias. Not all religious writings were chosen to be in the Bible. The Old Testament books—at least those felt to be suitable for Christians—were chosen to be in the Old Testament in the third century A.D. The acceptable books for the New Testament were chosen in the second century. Some of the ones rejected by the Old Testament selection committee were allowed to be included in the Apocrypha. (Most Bibles don't come with one; but if you find one, read it some day. It's full of marvelous stories; some of them would be "R" rated.)

The Bible is religious history. The facts aren't always accurate, but the meaning behind the story is. For example, it doesn't really make a lot of difference which nativity story you buy into because looking back from the empty tomb, both of them are saying the same thing. It was a very special birth.

As a religious history, as in any history, the Bible reflects the writer's bias. The author of the Gospel of Mark was trying to gather all the stories circulating about Jesus. Up to that point there were only a few written fragments about his life, plus many spoken (oral tradition) stories. Mark gathered what he could, and his edition was presented around 65 A.D. He put it together for the early church, which was starting to go through some heavy persecution.

Let's deviate for a moment and talk about oral tradition. It's important to understand how it happens in order to understand the development of the Scriptures. An event happens and is usually witnessed by more than one person. Each person who experiences that event is going to see it from his or her perspective. As each relates to the event, he or she is going to tell it from his or her point of view.

As an example, let's go back to my accident. One woman, in her seventies, who lived across the street from the firehouse, claimed that she saw the accident from her upstairs window. She also happened to be very friendly with the firemen. She said that the fire truck siren was going when the truck hit us and that Brad and I were driving fast and carelessly. When our attorney went to see the woman to take a deposition, he asked to see the window. She showed him, but he could not see the corner. Finally, he had one of his assistants hold him by his feet as he leaned out of the window. In this position he could get a tiny view of the corner where the accident happened. He confronted the woman with this, but she never relented. She swore that she saw the accident from that window.

My point is this: Sometimes, regardless of what really happened, people become locked into what they wanted to have happen. That can and does occur with oral tradition.

Let's look at another aspect of oral tradition. People hear a story. Each teller embellishes it just a speck. Over the years that story can change considerably. Let me share two stories about my father (an Episcopal clergyman who was a legend in his own time). He was an excellent preacher and packed the pews every Sunday. People liked to hear him preach because he told good stories and made rather strong statements about issues. He was not a wishy-washy person, and you either liked him or you didn't. Most of the "didn'ts" were other clergy who had a little professional jealousy.

The first story has to do with my father riding down the aisle of his church on Palm Sunday on a donkey. Supposedly, he did this every year to imitate Jesus' triumphal entry into Jerusalem. The second occurred shortly after he had arrived at this parish. The church had been having problems surviving, and it was his task to try and bring it back to life. So during the church service my father laid in an open casket and people filed by to view his body. When they looked down in the casket my father held up a mirror and they saw themselves. The moral: If that church was dying, it was because the members of the congregation were not doing what they should.

The reality is that these events did not take place. But I have heard these stories all over the world. People would swear on a Bible and be willing to bet money that these things really happened. I would try to tell people that they *never* happened, but they would not believe me. They wanted or needed to believe that my father had actually done these things. No amount of talking would convince them. I would try to tell them that my dad had a "palm procession" around the church on Palm Sunday, but no donkey. I would try to tell them that my dad told a *story* about a minister who put a mirror in a casket and had the congregation walk by— but it was only a story. It never happened that he laid in a casket.

Are you getting a picture here? Stories get started, people embellish them, change them, throw in their bias(es), and pass the story along as the truth. Do you think that something like this might have happened with the Bible? Let's go back to how the New Testament might have been formulated.

Approximately ten years after Mark compiled his edition, Matthew, using Mark's information, gathered other stories from different sources and wrote a Gospel designed to appeal to Jewish people. He had more information (it is the longest of the four Gospels) and wanted to share it with his fellow Jews. He was trying to say to them, "The long-awaited Messiah has come in the form of Jesus of Nazareth. Don't you see?" Then he proceeded to tell the story, using many Old

Testament quotations and background data to substantiate that the Messiah had come.

Ten years later Luke decided to write the story of the early church with more information and new sources. But he eliminated the Jewish slant and told it as a history of early Christianity. He also wrote the Book of Acts—the early history of the church. Now we don't really know if Mark, of the Gospel of Mark, or Matthew the tax collector, or Luke the doctor, or John the Apostle actually did the writing. Perhaps there were others who were smart businessmen or politicians, and after they had gathered the material and had written it, saw that their story would have more authority if the name of some bigwig in the early church was attached.

The Gospel of John was written about 110 A.D. during a time of heavy persecution. It was a very different book written to give hope to people who were paying the price (often their lives) for keeping the faith.

None of the authors appeared concerned with the facts. They told the stories in the way that best suited them, which incorporated their biases. As a result there are contradictions, inaccuracies, glaring mistakes, and inconsistencies with what went on in history at the time. Does that wreck it? Not for me. I love the fact that it was written by humans who had strengths, weaknesses, biases, and hang-ups—just like you and me. Just like I am writing this book with my biases.

Let's look at another matter that many people don't consider—the order of the books of the Bible. I think it's primarily because of the way the New Testament reads. It starts with Matthew, Mark, Luke, and John, the so-called Gospels. The Acts of the Apostles follows. (Acts really should be after Luke. After all, it is Volume 2 of his Gospel.) Then comes Romans—written by Paul. As a result of this order, many people have a tendency to believe that Paul came later after the Gospels were written.

Not so. Paul was dead and gone before the first Gospel was finished. That's right. Paul never had a Bible to wave around or quote from. Does that blow your mind? I have had people (guess who?) become furious with me when I have made this statement. They say, "That couldn't possibly be true because God arranged the Bible this way." Then they will show me Matthew, Mark, Luke, John, Acts, and so forth. After many years of trying to educate, I've learned just to be quiet. They don't want to be confused or threatened by the facts.

From the Book of the Acts of the Apostles and the letter of Paul, one can attempt to put together a biography of Paul starting at his conversion at about 35 A.D., five years after the crucifixion. He died some twenty-five years later in Rome.

In between a lot of travel, preaching, and harrowing experiences, Paul wrote some letters. Because of the content, the theology, the sophistication, and the style, one can generally place the letters in a different order from the listing one finds in the New Testament. Bible experts suspect that the second letter to the Thessalonians was Paul's first letter written about 48 A.D. Then came the first letter to the church in Thessalonia. The first letter to the church in Corinth was written about 54 A.D. The letter to the Galatians was written about the same time.

This is followed by an era called Paul's mature theology. His letters to the church in Rome (written from Corinth) happened about this time in 58 A.D. Soon after Paul went to Jerusalem; he was arrested and eventually sent to Rome where he awaited trial. In Rome, he wrote Colossians, Ephesians, and Philippians.

There are other letters reputed to have been written by Paul, but the literary style and content differ so from Paul's other letters that Bible scholars suspect another writer attached Paul's name to them.

I love that man Paul, even though at times he can be boring and some of his letters ramble on. I identify easily with his strengths and especially with some of his weaknesses; they're just like mine. Paul is a saint not because he was perfect but because he was so human, and at times, Destructive, yet continued to grow in the faith in spite of all the obstacles.

And what about the Old Testament? It's a religious history of Creation and of man's relationship with Creation—how some things worked and other things didn't. It's a story of how humanity continues to mess up and Creation continues to love and comfort us.

The Creation Story is beautiful. If one were to change each day into a millennium of years, one has a very scientific explanation of the evolution of creation and humanity.

The story of Eve coming from Adam's rib is fun. Unfortunately, it has had the tendency to make women viewed as second-class citizens. The story of Adam and Eve in the Garden is really the story of you and me, of all humanity. We are sitting in the lovely garden of life surrounded by beauty and creativity, and then we insist on being destructive.

The story of Cain and Abel sounds just like children getting ready to go to school or to church when they seem to want to kill each other.

One of my favorite stories is Noah and the Ark—a wonderful story. But most people miss the main point. There are some folks who run around the Middle East trying to find or dig up Noah's Ark. Others see it as a wonderful fable to share with their children. But they all stop before getting to the punch line of this myth. If you finish the story, the bad guys are drowned and no one is left but Noah and his God-loving/fearing family. What did Noah do? He went out, planted a vineyard, worked it hard, harvested the grapes, made wine (no, not grape juice), got drunk, laid naked in his tent, and passed out.[4]

Guess what? The one good guy succumbs to Destruction. It prevails. We can't drown Destruction. It's here to stay. It's part of our freedom—part of our humanity. There is no such thing as perfect. Separation is going to hang around forever. I love Noah because of his humanity.

The Old Testament is the story about Yahweh and humanity. Yahweh keeps trying to develop a loving relationship. The chosen are led out of slavery. Appreciative for a short time, the Israelites become Destructive (and unappreciative) when life becomes a little difficult. (Sound familiar?) But Yahweh keeps trying. Prophets try to warn and cajole. And just like today, people are turned off.

Moses comes down the mountain with the Ten Commandments, the first expansion of the basic law of love. By the time Jesus showed up, these ten laws had expanded to 613 laws. But all the legal wranglings that surrounded these laws only confused the Jews.

Pretty soon, the chosen people started loving the law (just like so many Old Testament Christians) and forgot Yahweh. It was a mess! What to do? Along came Jesus, the cross, and the empty tomb. Paul figured it out.

This is the Bible to me. I love it because of its truths. I read little bits of it on a daily basis. I also read many other books by inspiring, exciting, Christ-centered people. Some of these books are even better than the Bible. To me they say much more, especially more than the Book of Revelation. (See Appendix A, Obscene Words and Phrases.)

My heart bleeds for those who see the Bible as final and ultimate. Basically, it's only a guideline. For example, the Old

---

4. See Gen. 9:20–24.

Testament tells us how humanity has tried to love Yahweh. Some of the Bible can be terribly boring. (Try to read Leviticus and stay awake.) Some of it can be very confusing (Gospel of John). Some of it is extremely helpful in our daily journey (read Galatians). Some of it looks to me to be useless (see Obadiah); but it's there for our perusal. So are the myriad of books written about it that try to help us understand it better and to lead us through it.

The Bible is so much a part of our faith, but it's not *the Faith*. It's not our salvation. Our justification or salvation is in our faith that Jesus is our Christ. And please try to remember, if you're feeling offended, the early Christians had no Bible—no New Testament—and they are just as saved as you and I.

The Bible, just like us, is not perfect. It contains some bad news (Garden of Eden, Cain and Abel, Sodom and Gomorrah, Pontius Pilot, Judas, Herod, etc.), as well as the Good News. In the next chapter, let us look at some bad news. It will set the foundation on which to develop the Good News.

CHAPTER 7

The Bad News!

Three people from different parts of the country died at the same time. They all went to heaven and were met at the gate by St. Peter.

The first person was an architect. He said to the Saint, "I would like to come into heaven please." Replied Peter, "All in good time! But first you have to pass one small test. You have to spell 'God.'"

"Oh, that's easy," said the architect, "G-O-D." "Very good!" answered St. Peter. "You can come in." The second person was a rancher from Texas. He said, "I'd like to enter."

Replied Peter, "All in good time. But first I have a little test you have to pass. All you have to do is to spell the word 'God.'"

"Simple," said the Texan, "G-O-D."

"Very good," answered the Saint. "You can come in." The third person was an attractive businesswoman from New York. She approached Peter, "I would like to come in."

"Well," said the Saint, "you'll have to pass one small test."

This made the woman very unhappy. "Oh, come on now. I've had it rough all my life. Just because I'm a woman, I have had to fight for everything that I ever received. I've had to take lower pay, plus lots of sexual harassment from most of my male colleagues. I've been continually harassed by bosses, men, and jealous women. Now you're going to give me a hard time."

Peter looked at her and said, "But it's only a little test. Spell 'Tchaikovsky.'"

I LIKE THIS STORY for a variety of reasons:

1. It always makes me chuckle, even though I can never spell that name without looking it up.

2. The joke gives a stereotyped image of heaven. Most people associate heaven with St. Peter, gates, accountings, decisions about getting in, and so on.

3. It serves as a good introduction to this chapter. The "Bad News" is about death, both our final one (when the brain stops functioning) and the little ones we suffer on a daily basis. The three people who arrived at the gate symbolize the final death. The woman from New York exemplifies the daily deaths that she felt she suffered from being a woman and being in the business world. We all suffer these deaths both within ourselves and in our dealings with our fellow human beings.

I sincerely believe that death is our number one enemy if we are not prepared for it. It's Bad News because one way or another it's going to kill us, unless we find a way to triumph over it. (See the next chapter.) Let's look more closely at these two kinds of death.

Our final death is not a comfortable subject. Most people don't even want to talk about it much less deal with the subject. We give death code words. The person passed on, expired, passed away, or went to their maker. There is a reluctance to just say "Joe died." We don't want to talk about it with our children, our spouses, our parents, our attorneys, anyone. Relatively few people make detailed plans for death. The only way many people deal with it is when they are confronted by it. Someone near and/or dear dies and they have to face it at that moment. But it's also a time of great confusion, and most people don't really deal with it as much as move through it to get it out of the way. Others become so locked into the death of a loved one that they can't move on with their lives.

What do you think really happens when a human dies? Are there Pearly Gates? An official greeter? A spelling test? "Stay up" or "go down" decisions? We don't really know. But we do know that death is the only certainty in life. All of us are going to have to do it. In spite of that fact, most people don't want to die. Over the years, I have heard a variety of reasons for this, such as it could be very painful, especially if we are involved in a horrible accident, or we are afraid of the "unknown" behind the curtain of death. Maybe it's because we don't feel ready. There are more things we want to do or we are too young. Which direction am I going to go? Will I have to live near my ex-spouse, old boss, or nasty neighbor? I still don't know how to spell "Tchaikovsky." The unknown is always uncomfortable.

What are some of the images that people have of what is going to happen to them when they die?

1. Nothing. We die and either are put six feet under or they burn us up in a hurry (cremation) and spread the ashes.

2. We shall go to a place called purgatory and await a decision: up or down.

3. Someone is going to be at the gate greeting us, either Peter or the Benevolent Dictator. He will have a judge's hat on and a list in his hands, probably a very long one. For some it could be very, very, very long. The list is going to have on it all the nasty/naughty/rotten/mean/evil things that we have done during our lives. All of them! Yes, even the time you talked back to your mother, father, teacher, or police; cut school; said the "f" or "s" word; used God's name in vain; or thought bad thoughts. Then there is the heavier stuff: murder, wife/child abuse, an affair, or incest. What would be on your list?

For some Christians, these negative events are categorized as celestial demerits (versus celestial brownie points). Each negative event in life has demerits attached to it. Unfortunately, we don't know Peter's demerit point system. However, it might go something like this. An affair could be a minus five if your marriage is already on the rocks and it happens with an unmarried secretary. On the other hand, it could count for a minus twenty if your marriage appears to be fine, you have children, and your affair is with the boss' pregnant wife. If only we knew the point system! (Unfortunately, there is only one way to find out.)

Now let's look at the other side of the ledger—the "nice" things that we have done in our lives. That list is probably much shorter. Again, we have no idea what earns us celestial brownie points and what their values are. One is not sure whether holding doors open for ladies, remembering someone's birthday or anniversary, sending Christmas cards, or giving a peso to a Mexican beggar are worth any brownie points at all. Perhaps they are worth only one-hundredth of a point. We just don't know.

However, the church and the clergy sometimes can give one the impression that they know the system; maybe not the exact numbers, but what it is that is going to help get us "in." They might even suggest that going to church, singing in the choir, showing up for work days, teaching Sunday School, or stuffing envelopes is going to earn us some points. Going so far as to pay for a building, set up an endowment, or buy the organ or other big things could probably guarantee "no test" at the Pearly Gates. (The reality: the clergy and the church don't know any more about the point system than you and I. We'll tell you why later.)

So there we are watching the Saint tally our records: demerits versus brownies. The process ends. Peter's head nods. Trumpets blare. The long-awaited decision is announced—up or down? Or, if the Roman Catholic church is right, we could hang around in "neutral" in purgatory. Yes, this is a bit facetious; but in many people's thinking, it's right next to the truth.

There's a story about a notorious ne'er-do-well who died and was terrified about demerits. He had spent years carrying on in bars, chasing women, gambling, and carousing. Waiting at the Pearly Gates, he knew that he would have to pay the price. Finally, the doors open and Peter greets him with open arms. The man asks, "Are you sure you don't have me confused with someone else?" "Oh no," said the Saint. "Everyone is welcome here. We don't keep records. That's just a myth!" The man couldn't believe it. Then he saw a large group of people standing in a corner. Every few minutes they would start to cry then turn around and kick the posterior of whomever was closest to them. This process went on and on. Finally, the man asked Peter what was happening with that group? Why were they crying and kicking each other? "Oh them," said the Saint. "They all thought that we kept records."

Do you really think that someone is "up there" keeping records? Many Christians do.

There are also plenty of Christians who are convinced that there are not many people in heaven. The Benevolent Dictator only wants a limited number, just those who are almost perfect. Of course, all baptized babies get in immediately. Unbaptized babies go to "neutral." Only Christians have a chance of getting in. (Sorry Buddhists, Muslims, Hindus, Jews, Mormons, Jesus.) They think that heaven (all-white clouds and uniforms) is an exclusive place. It's just you and me and a few of our mutual best friends.Do any of these preconceived notions strike a bell in your thinking about the afterlife? Do you really think that any of this is true? Hang in there. The next chapter is going to take the Bad News of death and use the power of the Good News to turn it into a positive. This may sound strange because I consider death to be "Public Enemy Number One." However, I fervently believe and take great comfort in the fact that Jesus has prepared a place for us. And that is good news indeed!

Now let's look at our daily deaths. Let's start with the idea that life is not a rose garden. No, let's be positive and say that life *is* a rose garden, but with lots of thorns. Another way of saying this is that in spite of the wonderful Creation around us, we die deaths within ourselves as well as in our relationships with others. Let's be more specific.

We shall start with the deaths within ourselves. Consider what happens when you oversleep. Now you will have to pay a price on the freeway, maybe even be late to work (and the boss has already warned you about your tardiness). You start to become angry with yourself. You jump into the shower, and it takes forever for the hot water to come. You curse. Then you remember that you have to take the trash out before you leave. "Why didn't I do that last night?" Too lazy. Glued to the "idiot-box" watching some inane movie, breaking a promise not to do that anymore. You remind yourself that you always have a hard time sticking with promises.

You are out of the shower drying yourself and get disgusted by the blubber you see in the mirror. All because "I don't exercise. . . . I eat too much. . . . Back to the gym tomorrow. Gee whiz, I think it's been two months since I darkened its doors." You see that there are a few more gray hairs. And look, the wrinkles are deeper.

You jump into your clothes. They are wrinkled and stained, but there's no time to change. You have hardly been awake for fifteen minutes and already you have started the daily ritual of reminding yourself how weak and ineffectual you are as a human being. Don't feel bad—most people do this to themselves. This is what is called being dead to yourself. You don't even like, much less love, yourself.

The above example is just a microcosm of what many people put themselves through to validate that they are dead to themselves. Look at all the addicts who are dead to themselves—druggies, gamblers, overeaters, smokers, alcoholics, spendaholics, sexaholics, bulimics. These are all folks who are dead to themselves and have learned a way of avoidance so that they don't have to deal with themselves or their basic issue(s). This is Bad News when people don't like/love themselves and maybe even hate who they are. Stay with us—the Good News has the answer if you want to hear it.

Now let's deal with the deaths that we have in our relationships with others. Sometimes (perhaps even many times) these deaths are caused by the negative feelings we have about ourselves. Let's go back to our earlier example of you getting up in the morning. By the time you are dressed and have gone to the kitchen you are rather unhappy with yourself. Here comes your significant other not looking too spiffy either. The coffee isn't ready. You snap at her.

"Where's the coffee? You never have it ready when I need it in the morning!

"How come you didn't pick up the dry cleaning yesterday? Where's my lunch? What? You need money? Where's the twenty dollars I gave you last week? What do you think I am, the bank?

"Why aren't those damn kids up? They have responsibilities!

"Kids, you better get out of that bed before I come and get you out! Answer me!

"I don't like your tone! Wait 'til I get home tonight. I'll ground you for a month."

And off you go, not only dead to yourself, but also dead in your relationship with those around you.

Let's look at some other ways we can die in our relationships with others. If I were to zero in on the one thing that gets us into more trouble in our relationships, I would say that it's our pride. It's the deadliest word in the English language because it is so good at killing relationships. Webster defines pride as "An overhigh opinion of oneself; exaggerated self-esteem; conceit; haughty behavior resulting from this; arrogance."

Further down under "synonym" it says, "Pride refers to a justified or excessive belief in one's worth, merit, superiority, etc." I agree with most of this definition but have yet to witness "justified" pride.

My pride gets me into trouble. I might think that it's justified, but I bet that *you* probably wouldn't see it that way. My pride tells me all the time that I'm right and you're wrong. My pride stops me from listening to you. My pride will interrupt you, walk away from you while you're talking, call you a nasty name, do an obscene gesture, yell, use profanity, and become irrational since I know that because of my superior intelligence, my maleness, my louder voice, my ability to be able to cuss better and longer, my size, my tears, and my stronger threats I am right and *you* are "guess what?" Can you imagine dealing with someone like this? (I suspect some of you might say, "Yes, and I do it on a daily basis.")

Now if *my* pride treats you this way, I wonder what will happen to *your* pride. Do you think that it might behave in a similar fashion? I suspect that most of us will act and react in somewhat similar ways. We probably call our reaction by a different word such as "righteous indignation," "resentment," "hurt," "disgust," "upset," "alienation," or whatever your code word is. All are different words with different intensities but have pretty much the same meaning. We are angry, mad, furious, all brought on by our pride.

Try this for a thought. How would you like to have had a video camera taping while you were going through this process of anger brought on by pride. I cringe at the idea. I am certain that I wouldn't like it.

How do you become angry? Are you quiet and withdrawn? Do you retreat silently into your shell but inside you are like a volcano ready to explode? Do you "stuff it" or do you deal with your anger? Or are you the explosive kind? You let it all out. You kick, hit, put holes in walls, break things, beat up people, yell, scream, threaten, destroy. Then do you use something (alcohol, drugs, food, cigarettes) to try to make you feel better?

After you let it out, what do you do then? Forget it and move on? Keep bringing it up and working it over? Put the other person in the deep freeze by not talking to them for days on end? Become vengeful? Threaten them with some kind of awful action? Start keeping a list of all their past offenses? Do you deal Creatively or Destructively with your anger?

Another form of pride and a by-product of our anger is hatred—either of individuals or groups. Hatred is anger gone sour, not dealt with. It can destroy the lives of both the hater and the hated. While I was writing this book, the Los Angeles riots of 1992 occurred. The whole incident was based on hatred.

Whites hate Blacks. They keep them in poverty and have an army of police to make sure that the Blacks stay there. After two hundred years of this hatred, the Blacks can't take it any more and their hatred of being kept down explodes. People are killed and a part of the community is destroyed. People pretend that they are going to do something to help the poor get more jobs, rebuild the community, and receive better education, but the hatred (on both sides) is still there, maybe even a little more intense.

Let's try a little exercise to help us get in touch with our prejudice, anger, hatred, and pride. Many people say that they are not prejudiced, feel no anger toward others, and hate no one. This sounds good (especially if one is a Christian), but it is humanly impossible. Every human being has prejudices, is angry with someone or at something, and has hatred. Probably my biggest "hate" is toward people who hate, but it is still hatred. Most people have other words for prejudice, anger, and hatred, but the basic concept is there. Let's check it out. Go get your pencil and get ready to dig deep for *total* honesty.

PREJUDICES

Even if you only have a very small reaction or negative feeling toward any of the following items, write it/them down. We shall go back later and put a value on them.

1. Any race(s):

_____

This should include any group you refer to by another name (i.e., Hispanics—wetbacks, etc.).

2. Another religion:

_____

This includes cults and offbeat groups. (I score big on this one.)

3. Habits:

_____

Don't forget those nose pickers.

4. Nationalities:

_____

Now that the Russians are our friends we seem to be looking for a new scapegoat such as the Japanese or the Iranians. What are yours?

5. Physical characteristics:

_____

Tall vs. short; fat vs. thin; big nose vs. pug nose; long toes vs. stubby toes, etc.

6. Appearance:

_____

Sharp dresser vs. slob; tattooed; purple hair; pony tail vs. crew cut, etc.

7. Your own private "pet peeve(s)" (i.e., prejudices):

_____

_____

Now let's look at the things about which you might be angry (or disillusioned, disgusted, upset, bothered, annoyed, etc.). If in doubt about your word, look in a thesaurus. My computer thesaurus gives fifteen other words for angry and twenty-eight others for anger. Here is another list. I shall suggest a category; you fill in the blank with your word(s). (For example, Sibling: I am angry with my brother for teasing me when I was younger.)

A Race

_____

Relative

_____

Airline

_____

Store

_____

Parent

_____

Sibling

_____

Child

_____

Political Party

_____

Religion

_____

Church

_____

Minister

_____

Attorney

_____

Doctor

_____

A Business

_____

A Cause

_____

Neighbor

_____

Government Agency

_____

Your "special" anger

_____

Don't forget that all of the above can be in the plural (i.e., Races).

Now let's use the same list for your "hate(s)."

A Race

_____

Relative

_____

Airline

_____

Store

_____

Parent

_____

Sibling

_____

Child

_____

Political Party

_____

Religion

_____

Church

_____

Minister

_____

Attorney

_____

Doctor

_____

A Business

_____

A Cause

_____

Neighbor

Government Agency

Your "special" hate

Do your lists surprise you? Mine surprise me. The main point is that we often kid ourselves into thinking that we don't have prejudice, anger, or hatred. As a result, we don't deal with it, and it can sometimes get out of control.

On with the exercise. Let's use a scale of 1 to 10, with 1 being "very slight" and 10 being "extremely strong" with varying degrees in between. Example: You might feel like a "1" about your sister who angers you occasionally, a "5" about a cousin who is dishonest in business, but a "10" about a father who verbally and emotionally abused you. He could even slip over to a "1" or a "2" on your hate scale. Now go back and put a value on each of the above items you listed. Then write how many years you have felt that way. The final and hardest step is to review your lists and ascertain where your pride is involved in each of the items. Perhaps you are angry at your sister because she doesn't do things your way. Pride says, "I'm right! You're wrong!" About the dishonest cousin your pride says, "Your dishonesty is wrong! I don't think I'm dishonest, so therefore, I am right and you are a number 5 on my anger list."

The point of this whole exercise is to show how our pride can tie up our whole lives. It can control us so that we cannot function. It can prevent us from speaking the truth, keep us locked up in our house, stop us from answering the telephone, or drive us nuts. It can destroy us. Pride is truly bad news.

Now for a little exercise. Get a piece of paper. Divide it in half. On the left side write your list of the people with whom you are angry, at any level, using your favorite code word for anger. Using a scale of 1 to 10 ("1" being least angry and "10" being most angry), write down your degree of anger toward each person. Now write in a word or two as to why you are angry with him/her/them. Put down how many months or years you have been angry with that person. Then determine where *your* pride is with that situation. On the right side of the page make your list of the people (individuals and groups) whom you hate, the degree of your hatred, why you feel that way, how long you've felt that way, and how your pride is involved in the relationship.

Our pride can sure get in our way, can't it? Our pride is Bad News because it can cause us to die in our relationships with others. How does your list look? Long and threatening?

Consider these other forms of pride that get in the way of healthy, happy relationships.

How about jealousy or envy? It's a form of pride built on a lack of self-esteem. We become jealous of someone else's body (or looks, successes, possessions, money, etc.) because we don't feel good about ours. We are not happy where we are; therefore, our pride looms forth because we want to be where they are. For some reason, we think we deserve what they have.

For example, we think that money is going to bring us happiness. We buy lottery tickets so that we can win and be happy. For so many of us, happiness and ownership seem to go together. If only I can have the new car, house, boat, or dress, then I'll be happy. Because the odds are about one in 14 million of winning in the state lottery, most of us have not won. But our neighbor, who one time bought a $1 ticket, won $5 million. We go nuts. Our pride and our jealousy go wild because we know that we should have won. We deserve it, and we feel estranged from the winner. Bad News prevails.

Our anxiety is built on pride. Anxiety is based on a fear of what might happen, not what is really happening. We lose our job and immediately become concerned that we might lose our house, our car, and our possessions. What will people think about us as we push our shopping cart down the street? People will make fun of us. Our friends will abandon us. We won't be able to get a job because we won't be able to shower and put on fresh clothes. Our pride will be destroyed.

Every anxiety that we have is built around our pride. We are afraid of losing self-worth. People won't like us if such and such happens. Our self-esteem could go down the tubes, and we would feel worthless, dead to ourselves as well as others.

The most delicious form of pride is the phrase "I told you so." I cringe when my wife says or implies that. I don't want to hear that at all. My pride wants me to be right, and I don't like to hear her tell me "You're wrong." It's like the man sitting at the bar getting plastered and the bartender asks, "What's wrong?" He replies, "Well, my wife kept telling me to ask the boss for a raise. I keep putting if off and she kept after me. Finally, today I got up the nerve and asked. You know what? I got the raise." The bartender, perplexed, says, "Congratulations. But why are you so unhappy?" Responds the man, "Now I have to go home, tell my wife I got the raise, and hear her say 'I told you so.' " Oh how our pride hates to hear those words.

The very worst kind of pride is the pride of thinking that one understands pride and is immune from it. Sometimes people use humility as a way to cover their pride. I am rather suspicious of humble people and often wonder if their humility isn't a form of pride. A clergy friend of mine summarizes this idea very succinctly when he says, with tongue in cheek, "The very best sermon I ever preached was on humility."

I do not even try to start to understand my pride. I do know that it is part of my human condition. It comes out at the darndest times and does the darndest things. It gets me into trouble time and time again. It's responsible not only for the deaths that take place between me and my fellow human beings, but also for the deaths that take place between me and me. Pride is Bad News. Death, both the daily ones and the final one, is also Bad News, unless I can do something creative about it.

Let's move on to chapter 8 where your long-awaited answers can be found.

CHAPTER 8

Now the Good News!

Two little boys are walking, deep in conversation.

"You know," one of the little boys says, "nothing lasts forever. All good things must come to an end."

The two of them think about his statement for a few minutes. Finally, the second boy turns to the first one and asks, "When do the good things start?"

NOW. NOW. We are going to start talking about the Good News.

As we go back to the story of Jesus, it does not sound like Good News. The fact is that things are rather bleak. According to Scripture, five days earlier Jesus had been received into the city of Jerusalem as the "Son of David . . . who comes in the name of the Lord!" (Matt. 21:9). Some saw Jesus as the long-awaited Messiah. Now the Son of David is hanging on two pieces of wood in a place called Golgotha (translated "skull"). It's not a nice place because the Romans did their executing there—as many as three hundred in one day.

The heat of the high desert sun is beating down on Jesus and the other two criminals hanging there with him. He is considered a criminal because some people said that he claimed to be a king (completely unacceptable in the Roman Empire). These trumped-up charges were one way people (or entities) dealt with threats to their power. Crucifixions were a common occurrence. Jesus didn't last very long, dying within three hours.

During his ministry, Jesus had made contact with a respected member of the Sanhedrin, Judaism's ruling body, named Joseph of Arimathea. Joseph, fearing that Jesus' body might be thrown on the flaming trash heap (known as Gehenna), decided to obtain the body and give it a decent burial.

Here's an interesting thought: Suppose Joseph had not obtained the body of Jesus, and after he was dead, the Romans simply threw it on the hot fires of Gehenna and it burned? Would there have been a resurrection?

Remember, Jesus was put on the cross at approximately noon on Friday and was dead by about 3:00 P.M. The Roman authorities allowed the influential Joseph to take the dead body. He had to move quickly to finish putting Jesus in the tomb before sundown, the start of the Jewish Sabbath and the Passover. Because he lacked the time, the correct anointing and preparation would have to happen on Sunday morning after the Sabbath ended (at sundown on Saturday). Still, there is nothing in this story that is unusual. A man dies and is buried.

Here comes the part upon which I feel Christianity is based. Without the next event, Jesus would have been just another rabble-rouser who tangled with the power structure and "disappeared." History would not have recorded the incident or even the life of this poor Jewish peasant.

Close friends of Jesus were concerned not only with what had happened to their leader on Friday but also that his body had not been given a proper burial. On Friday evening, after the body was entombed, a group of religious leaders, with Pilate's permission, took a contingent of soldiers to seal the tomb with a huge rock. They stayed there around the clock to make certain that nothing happened to the body.

When a group of followers arrived early Sunday morning to anoint the body, the guards were gone, the huge stone protecting the entrance had been rolled back, and someone was sitting in the tomb telling the followers that Jesus "is not here . . . He has risen. . . (Matt. 28:6). Why do you seek the living among the dead? . . (Luke 24:5). He is going to Galilee. . . You will see him" (Mark 16:7).

Can you imagine going to a tomb site and having that happen to you? Luke says it for me, "They were afraid" (24:5). But scary or not, to me this is the heart of Christianity. Without the empty tomb, Jesus is no different from any other itinerant preacher. Everything else he did has been done as well, if not better, by others. History has given us better preachers, better miracle workers, better charismatics, better Christians (Jesus never was one), and better humans. But no one else bested death. That tomb was empty. He was gone. He died but is now "alive." He overcame the finality of death.

Now let's translate this into action. Our antagonist is *death*—both our final one and our daily ones. Death keeps confronting me. I am more than sixty years old. My average "life span" gives me about 18 more years, but I learned a long time ago that there can be a fire engine around every corner. That death is waiting is not a comforting feeling. Also, I know that somehow, somewhere, sometime within the next

24 hours, I shall probably die a death in relationship to myself and maybe with another human being. Again, not a good feeling. But I have met a man who has conquered death, and even though he died, he lives.

I want to be able to do this: to die and yet continue to live. I want a plausible explanation about my final death and ways of dealing creatively with my daily deaths. Jesus is going to give me some answers about that which I fear the most: death.

At this point, I need to try to answer that inevitable question: How do I know that the tomb was really empty? A very quick answer: I don't really know.

There are no photographs, videotapes, newspaper articles, or even first-hand witnesses who saw him leave. Jesus' followers had no idea the tomb was empty until they arrived to anoint the body. Perhaps the guards knew it, but we shall never know.

Maybe someone paid off the guards and they stole the body. It's a thought, but who would want it? The Romans, the Jewish leaders, the Herodians all wanted this rabble-rouser out of the way. The last thing they would have wanted was for that body to be stolen. It would reek of martyrdom, and a riot would ensue. Just keep the body in the tomb and the troublemaker would soon be just a memory.

Perhaps some of Jesus' disciples stole his body. I suspect, however, that after they saw how quickly the religious leaders got rid of Jesus (in less than 24 hours), the close followers went into hiding for fear that they would be next. Anyway, they were all good Jews who would not break the Sabbath—even to steal the dead body of their leader.

Some have suggested that maybe the disciples were hallucinating. People sometimes do that after the death of someone very close. They swear that they see or hear or communicate with the dead person. Remember my friend

Brad who was killed on the murdercycle? I have seen Brad at least half a dozen times since his death in 1958—at least my imagination has conjured him up. Of course it wasn't Brad but my imagination going wild. Maybe because of the intimate relationship that these people had with Jesus, their imaginations went wild, and they only thought that they saw him, talked with him, walked with him, or had breakfast with him. But this is *not* what they said.

Another theory is that Jesus didn't really die on the cross; he just fainted or swooned (a partial loss of consciousness). Because sophisticated medical equipment wasn't available, the centurion who was guarding Jesus beneath his cross thought, from Jesus' vital signs, that he was dead. So the centurion ordered the body taken down. According to this theory, Jesus wasn't really dead, just unconscious when they took him inside the cool tomb and laid him on a damp, cold rock where he revived. Interesting concept. I can't refute it, but I can suggest that if it were ever discovered that Jesus wasn't really dead, the centurion would have been crucified himself. My military background says the centurion wasn't going to risk that. My belief is that Jesus was dead, deader than a doornail.

I have no positive proof. I don't need it. However, I am not certain that an actual photo, or even a live interview with an on-the-spot witness, would convince people who don't want to believe that the Resurrection really happened. Before they can believe, people, either consciously or unconsciously, have to be looking for a new christ. Their old one isn't working.

I was in my early twenties and in the Marine Corps when I discovered that my old christs did not do the job. You might ask, "Like what old christs?" My answer would be, "My self-centeredness, my wanting to party, treating women as second-class citizens, my 'I couldn't care less' attitude." This attitude was creating some real problems concerning my future in the Corps. Daily, I was dying—deaths within myself and with my fellow human beings. I was ripe for a new christ. Fortunately, I was brought up in the church, and some of the seeds sown in my first seventeen years— although some landed on hard, rocky soil—some did germinate. They were sitting there waiting for me to farm them. So there I was, twenty-one years old, not feeling good about my life, and looking for a new christ. Because of my early involvement with the church, I was semiliterate about Christianity. Some of it started to make a degree of sense, and at that stage, I was at least willing to listen to (maybe not accept) the idea of the Resurrection.

It was after a half-dozen years of front-line ministry that the truth of the Resurrection came to me: It does not really make any difference whether the Resurrection actually took place or not. It can never be proven. It is based primarily on a "leap of faith."

The power of the Resurrection is not in what *actually* happened on that first Easter (because no one really knows). *Its power lies in what the very idea of Resurrection can do to a person, a group, or a community.* I have witnessed individual lives change drastically, not because someone had a picture proving that Jesus arose from the dead but because they saw or felt the power of the Resurrection in others. They knew that they must "die to the past" so that they could arise to a new life. The drug addict who has been strung out for years cannot make any changes until she realizes that her old christ isn't working. She must die to that old life before she can sober up and arise to a new life.

At one time in my life, I was the program director of a drug treatment center. On almost a daily basis, I saw the Resurrection in action as people detoxed from their old christ and started a new drug-free life.

In marriage counseling, I have seen couples dead to each other (and to themselves) die to their old lives of being critical, self-serving, mean, and abusive. Realizing their behavior toward each other was terrible, they wanted a change. They started doing nice things for the other person, learned how to curb their tongues, complimented each other, told the other person on a daily basis that they loved them and started having weekly dates. They fell back in love. They made a new beginning, a new life. Resurrection.

I have shared the story about my father supposedly lying in a casket during a church service. As I said, that story was not the truth. It is true that my dad told a similar story. A group of church members whose church was dying walked past an open casket sitting in front of the altar one Sunday morning to look at the corpse of the dead church. As they looked in, they saw themselves because the pastor had placed a mirror where the body would have been. The point: The church was dead because the people were dead. Now the rest of the story.

In 1936, my father accepted an invitation to become rector (senior pastor) of a dying parish on the outskirts of Philadelphia. Urban flight had started. The previous rector had stayed too long and had become ineffectual. Church members were losing interest. It was a challenge, but my father knew that with the power of Creation, he could resurrect that church. He initiated new programs: Sunday worship became exciting, a magnificent choir was developed, the preaching was outstanding, it became an integrated parish, and it became involved in the life and issues of the community. Eventually there was standing room only every Sunday, even in the hot, humid Philadelphia summers. Life out of death. This is the power of the Resurrection. This is the power of that simple Jewish peasant who was *not* in the tomb when he was supposed to be.

On and on we could go with stories about new life out of death, but stories are not our objective here. What we want to emphasize is that regardless of what really happened on that first Easter, over the centuries its power has become unbelievable. The course of civilization has changed dramatically. This moment in time is referred to as the bridge between B.C. and A.D. Millions of lives have been transformed. People and their needs have been addressed. Schools have been started, hospitals built, slavery abolished, and shelters created for unwed mothers, senior citizens, orphans, runaways, drug addicts. So many service opportunities have been created in the name of the "rabble-rouser" who taught us how to make life out of death.

Are you looking for a new christ? Are you ready for a new christ?

Let's look more closely at Jesus. I see him as being able to do a series of things for us.

1. He will start the process of bringing us into a *new* relationship with the Creator and Creation.

2. This relationship is built on love—unconditional love. We are, and will continue to be, loved in spite of ourselves. No matter what we do or how society labels us, the love will continue to flow as long as we allow it.

3. We shall open ourselves up so that Creation will start to flow into and through us. We shall learn how to be lovers, how to forgive, dump guilt, accept people as they are, and on and on.

4. We shall learn how to "do" Resurrection (die and rise to new life) with ourselves and with others on a daily basis.

5. Death—the fear of it, the negativity of it—will no longer have dominion over us. We know how to do Resurrection, and we know that there is life after life.

One weekend my wife and I were skiing at Mammoth, about a six-hour drive from where we lived. It was a beautiful day, and even though we had planned to start home about 1:00 P.M., we kept skiing until 4:00 P.M. We started the long trek home and about 9:00 P.M., in the middle of nowhere, the car ran out of gas. About one thousand yards away was a federal prison. In the dark and cold, we stood outside the car hoping someone would stop. Cars whizzed by for an hour not even slowing down. Finally, a car drove by, slowed down, did a U-turn, and came back. It was a young woman alone.

"What's the problem?"

"Ran out of gas. We need a ride to the nearest gas station."

"Hop in and I'll take you," the woman replied.

And she did, twenty miles away. After we got the gas, she then drove us back to our car and waited until we poured it in and made sure the car started. We felt that that woman was a "lifesaver." She didn't really save our lives, but because of her kindness, trust, and generosity she made it possible for us to continue our journey.

I see Jesus as a "lifesaver." He is going to provide the tools so that we can keep moving through life. Many Christians would probably use a different phrase such as Jesus is their Savior. I don't have a problem with that except that I am not quite sure that it really describes what Jesus is going to do for us. So I prefer to use the phrase "lifesaver."

This phrase also helps me to avoid an uncomfortable question that some "churchie" folks ask because I really don't know how to answer it: "Am I saved?" The real question is, "Am I a Christian?" I am never sure why they didn't ask me that second question in the first place. But every time someone asks me that, I feel that there is really a series of hidden questions such as "Am I a fundamentalist?" "Do I believe that God wrote the Bible?" "Do I go to church twice on

Sunday and once on Wednesday?" "Do I consume fermented grape juice or harder stuff?" "Have I memorized Scripture?" "Do I speak in tongues?"

There are probably more innuendos in the question, "Are you saved?" I feel that if I answer no to any of the above questions the other person will say aloud or silently that I am not *really* a Christian or at least not a real Christian. Obviously, then I am not saved. (All this is fine with me because if that is what it takes to be saved, count me out.)

I don't think that Jesus can really save me from anything. Is he going to save me from making mistakes? No. I seem to make as many being a Christian as I did before. Save me from going to hell? No, because I can't be saved from a place that isn't there. Save me from becoming separated from my fellow human beings? No, because I am a human being who suffers like every other human from broken relationships.

Is Jesus going to save us from being an alcoholic, having an affair, being mean? No, because as long as we have the freedom to pick and choose, we are going to continue to eat the forbidden fruit. As long as we have freedom, we shall continue to do destructive things to ourselves and others.

Is Jesus going to save me from my final death? No way. It's the *only* thing in life besides taxes on which I can count.

I really don't want to be saved. Rather, I want a "life-saver," a christ who can give me the tools to be able to triumph over death. (There is one exception: I really do want to be saved from having people ask me if I am saved.) There is an old Chinese proverb: "Give me a fish and I eat for a day. Teach me to fish and I fish for a lifetime." I want Jesus to teach me to fish.

Now that I have found a workable christ—Jesus—how can I become more involved in life? The church says that one has to be baptized first. This involves a ritual that I have suggested can vary greatly from denomination to denomination and then vary further within each church. Most say that baptism can be done only by a "chosen" few (clergy) who know how to do it. These "chosen" will then dogmatically state where and how it must be done. Some say that it will "take" if you sprinkle only a few drops of special water on the person's head. Others want to get you into a large body of water and hold you under until you think that you are going to meet your "maker" sooner than you thought. Once is enough a few churches say. Some people like to be baptized lots of times. They think each baptism earns celestial brownie points. The baptism debate goes on and on.

These great theological issues obviously consume a lot of time in the church, but frankly, I don't feel that they are even worth discussing. Let's go back to the first followers of Jesus. There is no indication they were baptized. If they weren't baptized, what do you think has happened to them? Have they been relegated to an eternity in hell?

Jesus was baptized, but it was not the same as our baptism. His was done by his cousin, John, in the river Jordan. It was more a symbolic act of cleansing. John was big on "repenting" and felt that life would not go well for Israel until all of the Jews cleansed themselves in the river Jordan. One suspects that it was not a very popular movement. John lost his head over it, and Jesus didn't talk about it.

Baptism in the Christian church is analogous to the Good News. As Jesus died on the Cross and then arose from the dead, we too, in baptism, die to our lives separated from Creation and during the process of baptism arise to new life with Creation.

Let's try a word picture. Envision a telephone. It's in a store waiting to be purchased. Even though it looks like a telephone and is called a telephone, it is not functioning as a telephone. Until it is connected to a telephone line, it is simply a piece of equipment. We are like that telephone before our baptism. We are disconnected from Creation. We are alive but not functioning near our potential. We seem to be doing okay, but we are not connected with the source of life.

Back to the telephone. Let's buy it and take it home. It's still not functional. We call the telephone company. They have been awaiting our call. "Will you connect us?" (baptism). "Of course we will" (Creation), and it's done. Now we plug in the telephone and we are connected.

Once you and I are connected, we now have a direct line to Creation. We don't need any middlemen, e.g., clergy, church, prophets, swamis. We can do everything directly.

Baptism is even easier than buying a telephone. We simply have to say that we want to be connected, and it happens. The church probably won't tell you this, but you can baptize yourself. You don't need water. You don't need to say a word. The only thing you do need is to silently think "I want Jesus as my Christ." At that point, you are one of us. Welcome! Frankly, I think it's more enjoyable to be baptized with other Christians around to help you celebrate your new beginning.

A final thought. I am not sure why, but many Christians think that their kingdom is exclusive—only the right people doing the right things can enter. Maybe that is the way in their kingdom. The kingdom to which I belong is all-inclusive; the more the merrier. Creation welcomes gays, divorcees (it doesn't matter how many times), drunks, drug addicts, murderers, child abusers, pedophiles, wife beaters, fornicators, adulterers, those who are disabled, and even your cranky neighbor. That is what the Good News is all about—everyone is welcome if they want in. Welcome Jews, Muslims, Hindus, Mormons, and more, and you too, Jesus. I'll bet that's not the way you heard it in your church.

In the comic strip "B.C.," B.C. is climbing up the mountain to visit the Great Guru. At the top, he asks, "Oh, Great Guru, what is faith?" Guru ponders for a few moments and then replies, "Faith is a condemned prisoner asking for a doggie bag during his last meal." What is your faith about?

What makes sense to me, what my faith is about, is that the tomb was empty. Jesus prevailed over death. If we want him for a christ, he will show us how to conquer death and live forever. When I say live forever, I'm not saying we actually go somewhere. I don't believe there is an actual place with St. Peter, his checklist, and the Pearly Gates. Nor do I believe that we live on as a "soul" (see Appendix A, Obscene Words and Phrases). There really is no good answer to how and where we go—it's all part of the mystery of death. The only answer Christians have is that Jesus is going to prepare a place for us, and I feel that the part of us that lives on is the sum of all our individuality and uniqueness.

So how do we get started? Just say "I want Jesus for my Christ," and we are in business.

Now, let's look at how we can make this Good News work for us on a daily basis.

CHAPTER 9

Winning
with At-one-ing

THE GOOD NEWS IS that the tomb was empty. Jesus was victorious over death.

The Better News is that you and I can have the same victory over the daily deaths (separations) that we have with ourselves and with each other, as well as victory over our final death. The price? We must simply say that we want Jesus as our Christ. Once we do that, the process begins. But how does this work?

Let's start with a word and develop some images. The church calls the process "Atonement." I like to break the word down so that it looks like this: At-One-Ment. This is when we become at one with ourselves, our neighbors, and Creation. Unfortunately, this is not as easy to do as it is to say, but it's not that difficult if we are willing to bury our pride. The opposite of at-one-ment is un-at-one-ment, which is very easy to do and is the state that many of us seem to be in quite often. It's just part of our human condition. I become unhappy with myself for the things I do or the things I don't do and should. I can also become unhappy with you, or you with me, and then we are un-at-one. (Review chapters 1 and 7 to see how un-at-one we can become.) How do we go from un-at-one to at-one? I call the process "winning with at-one-ing."

Let's go back to the idea that when we come into the world we are un-at-one (separated) from Creation. We are born free to pick and choose whether or not we want to be a part of Creation. This does not mean that we are not important or unloved. It simply means that we are free. The choice is ours.

We can stay separated for the rest of our lives or we can become connected. It's our choice. How do we become connected? Through the simple act of saying that we want to be connected. The Church calls this "baptism" (an outward expression of an inner feeling). When that happens we receive four gifts:

1. We are connected directly to Creation. There are no middlemen.

2. Creation/Creativity flows directly through us; but we do have to be patient as we learn how to do this. It's going to take time.

3. *All* our separations, some of which can be very destructive, are forgiven just for the asking.

4. We shall live forever. Not in this body; but our individuality and uniqueness shall be preserved forever.

These four gifts used creatively can not only alter our lives but also add a dimension that we never thought possible.

Back to baptism. Remember, it's simply an act. Some people have an expectation that great miracles will happen immediately: life will become easy, things will start to make sense, or they will live in a euphoric state, protected from all the world's evils. From my vantage point that is not what happens. Perhaps one might feel very good while the baptismal ceremony is occurring or for a short while afterward, but I can assure you that reality returns very quickly. The challenges of life will keep coming our way, and some of those challenges will likely be difficult.

Another way of saying this might be that baptism is *not* a process of protecting people from the real world. Rather, it's the start of a journey that will teach people how to deal with the real world (good and bad) in a creative manner. Let me also assure you that it is not a quick fix. It will take a lifetime and then some to become proficient in learning how to take un-at-one-ment and turn it into at-one-ment.

Let's go back to our friend from Nazareth. He says the *only* answer is love. His people had tried everything to stay in a relationship with Yahweh, but none of it worked. Ever since Moses, Jewish people thought that the law was the answer. At the time of Jesus, his people had those 613 laws to follow in order to be at-one with Yahweh. That is a lot of laws for a person to remember. People forgot, misinterpreted, ignored, or played with the laws and became so entrenched that they lost perspective. The law became more important than Yahweh or love. Laws and love do not work well together. The law seems to constantly undermine love. (Unfortunately, many of today's Christian churches have two to three times more laws than existed at the time of Jesus.)

Jesus found his people much more into the law than into loving fellow human beings. He reminded them of what had been said centuries before in the books of Deuteronomy (6:5) and Leviticus (19:34), that love is the answer, specifically to "love self, neighbor, and God." And with love and Creation also comes freedom.

Most human beings have a difficult time with freedom. We feel much more secure living under the law than under freedom. In my many years of working with adolescents, I found that we, the church, could offer a great experience to young people by taking them to a conference center for a forty-eight to seventy-two-hour period and providing them with a multitude of experiences, i.e., camaraderie, worship, campfires, study sessions, and a taste of freedom. We called these experiences "freedom camps." This meant that for the time we were together the only law would be the law of love—self, neighbor, and Creation. There would be no other laws. They would not have to come to teaching sessions, worship, campfires, meals, anything. But for every choice that they made they would have to answer these questions:

- Whatever I do, will I still love me?
- Will I love my neighbor and will my neighbor still love me?
- What would Creation think of my choice?

Of course they ran the gamut of abuse, staying up all night (this was the biggie at least for the first night) and missing sessions or worship. Some would try to bring drugs or alcohol to camp. (For the most part, however, their contemporaries policed each other because they liked the idea of freedom camps and did not want some "druggie" to wreck it for them.) A few used the camp experience for "making out" time, and some simply slept the entire time.

In the Marine Corps, I learned that about ten percent of any given population is going to mess it up for the others because of their bad behavior. It was true at freedom camps, with the clergy, on boards of directors, and in my fraternity, as well as in other places. In terms of the freedom camps, about ten percent of the clergy wanted to put me on a cross for allowing young people to experience the idea of Christian freedom.

We did evaluations at the end of each camp, and one of the universal responses was "Freedom camps are very difficult because *I* have to make choices that I never have had to make before. It's much easier to live under the law than under freedom and love." I still find this true in all aspects of life. People would rather live under the law. Freedom isn't easy!

My own church has a whole book of laws called "Canon Law." It has about three times (more than 1,700) as many laws as Jesus had in his day. As humans, we have a tendency to migrate toward the law and away from love. Take, for example, the issue of gays being first-class citizens. Because so many church folks have homophobia, it seems to be much easier to pass laws making sure that gays remain second-class Christians than to love and accept them as fellow human beings and believers.

As a result, gay priests, bishops, and Christians often are forced to remain "underground" so that they can be part of a "loving community." How hypocritical and dishonest, but the church with its version of the truth insists on the law.

Churches seem to distrust freedom and tend to become very legalistic. Unfortunately, after two thousand years, not much has changed. We now have new categories of undesirables, more laws, and not much of a superabundance of love.

It is important, at this time, to look more deeply at what Jesus was saying when he spoke about love. Jesus was lucky—in his language (Aramaic or "street" Greek versus classical Greek), there were four different words for love. Unfortunately, in English there is only one word to express the love we have for our significant other, child(ren), parents, dog, car, favorite ice cream, or whatever. One might love them all, but I hope with a much different degree of intensity. The Aramaic/Greek language used four different words.

The first kind of love is "philia" (like Philadelphia, the city of brotherly love), which is a love that exists between friends, perhaps us and our pets, and maybe even us and "things." This kind of love requires something in return such as acknowledgment, caring, or involvement. Without something in return, "philia" isn't going to last very long.

Next is "storge," the affection among parents, children, siblings, and relatives. Sometimes there is not a lot of "like" in this love, but when push comes to shove, most of the time family will stick up for each other. *I* can tell you what bad news my brother is, but I don't want to hear it from *you*. Remember, blood is thicker than water. Again, storge expects something in return (or people start talking about disinheriting).

Then there is "eros," or erotic love, which is the love that exists between husband and wife or between lovers. Obviously, it is a deeper love with a great deal more of our emotions involved. Our sensuality and sexuality are included, but again we need something in return if we are to continue eros.

The fourth kind of love is different. It's called "agape." It's a love that expects nothing in return. It's a love given to us by Creation primarily because we are a part of it—a very important part. It's given freely, *if* we want it. There are no strings attached. Even if we are Destructive, we are still given this love.

One can't earn agape nor can it be purchased, pleaded for, or cajoled. It doesn't need to be; it's free! Remember, there are no celestial brownie points, so good works count for naught when it comes to receiving agape.

The love that Jesus wants us to share entails accepting people the way they are. He loved the lepers of his day, both the literal ones as well as the figurative ones such as tax collectors, women of ill-repute, the mentally/physically sick, the wealthy, the poor, and even Gentiles. Our love can know no boundaries. It can't be judgmental of people or they will end up on the exclusion list. It's so easy to judge others if they are not like us. But let me share a secret: judging others, encouraging our own little prejudices, and making other people the "bad guy" take a lot of hard work and really tie up our lives.

Suppose that you have a prejudice toward obese people. Wherever you go, you are going to find people with that problem. So every time you see an obese person your negative thoughts kick in and you go through your litany about why fat people are disgusting. Wouldn't it be easier just to turn that prejudice off immediately and pick out a positive trait of that person on which to focus? The Good News is that we only have to love people, not judge them, hate them, or develop negative feelings toward them.

Love is different from "like." Sometimes, as Christians, we confuse love and like. We have a tendency to see Christianity as a popularity contest: We have to like everyone and everyone has to like us, and *then* we shall enter the Pearly Gates. That's not how Jesus saw it. There were many people he didn't like and quite a group who didn't like him. But he *loved* them. Dying on his cross he said, "Father, forgive them for they know not what they do" (Luke 2:34). I interpret this as "I don't have to like you, but I do have to love you and accept you as you are."

I also have to forgive you because forgiveness is the foundation upon which this love is built. For me to carry hatred, vengeance, animosity, anger, or hostility toward you, no matter what you did, will more than likely destroy me before it destroys you. Why? Because I will start to center my life around what you did or didn't do. I'll think about it constantly. I'll work myself into a lather about it. Maybe I won't sleep at night, or perhaps I shall want to sleep too much. Perhaps I'll stop eating or maybe I'll eat all of the time. Whatever! But the last person in the world that I would want to have control of me—you—now has control. Isn't it easier to forgive and move on?

Jesus says it is. Forgive once? "No," says he. "Forgive three times?" "No, not three times . . . but seventy times seven" (Matt. 18:22). That's a whole lot of forgiving, but it also keeps us "clear" and ready to move on. (Fundamentalists take note: 7x70 does not mean 490 times. It means infinity. I sometimes have the mental image of a literal fundamentalist carrying around a little black book, keeping score. When the 491st offense happens, one no longer has to forgive.)

Jesus' idea of love includes the terrible, painful process of having to bury one's pride and saying "I'm sorry"—and mean it. Some people keep saying it but don't really mean it. Other people won't say it because they see it as a form of capitulation and weakness. For example, when I tell you that I am sorry for something, that means I'm wrong and you're right, that I lost and you won. That will mean that you are better than I am and can tell me what to do. That means that you will probably tell me to do awful things that I don't want to do. So why should I tell you that I am sorry? There seems to be a whole bunch of unwritten rules about saying "I'm sorry." But Jesus' idea of love doesn't have to go through that horrible process. It simply says "I'm sorry" and moves on with life.

This loves says to forget guilt! As we have said before, guilt is only going to bog us down. So let it happen for about five seconds, then nail it to the cross and let it die there as you go ahead with your Creative life.

Repentance is a part of this love. Repentance does not mean having to put more money in the offering plate, or crawling down the aisle on our knees, or paying for the building of a cathedral. It means to turn our lives around. Say "I'm sorry," "You're forgiven," "Let's start over," "Love, not hate," and on and on. With this, you can have your

Easter, life, at-one-ment, heaven, togetherness. This is winning with at-one-ing.

I strongly believe that practicing the law of love is the main task of a Christian. The process starts with "me." I have to love "me" before I can really love "you." I have to do it very quickly because the longer that I allow negativity to dominate my life, the more I allow life to suppress me. Paul says it very succinctly: "Do not let the sun go down on your anger" (Eph. 4:26).

This love says that separation is a part of life and living. It's okay to be separated. It's a part of our humanity. But we have to move through it because to hang on to it will be destructive to us and to our fellow human beings. As believers and followers of Jesus, let's take the cross and push through the pride, say "I'm sorry" or "You're forgiven," and move on with our lives.

At this point, death no longer has dominion over me. By moving through the separation, I have removed the death that exists between you and me. I am now free to be at one with me, you, and Creation. *This is Easter.* We have conquered death and can rise to new life free and clear, at least for now. We can do it all over again because separation keeps happening. We have to move through the process very quickly. At some point, after a lot of trial and error, we become rather adept at the process. What a feeling. This is really Good News. And do you know what? It costs nothing. It's ours for the asking. What a deal! I *can* get to heaven without going to church.

Whenever I suggest that we are saved by our faith and our faith alone (versus something else such as perfection, good works, being "nice" or politically correct) most people just don't buy it. It's too easy.

But I did not invent this—honest. It's in the Bible. Paul was the master designer of this doctrine. As he grew and matured as a Christian, he came to grips with the fact that one can *not* earn one's salvation. It is a gift given to us through the work of Jesus on the cross and the empty tomb. The passages in Appendix B substantiate this basic Christian doctrine.

I know this sounds much too easy, but it is the only way that salvation is going to happen. According to the Old Testament, people tried all kinds of other ways to stay at one with the Creator. They all failed. However, being saved by our faith has lasted for two thousand years, so one would have a tendency to believe that it is here to stay.

Let's take a look at what to do with our telephone line once it's connected to Creation (i.e., prayers).

CHAPTER 10

Let Us Pray

Discovering at the last minute that the minister had forgotten to invite an elderly parishioner to his garden party, he hastily telephoned her. "It's too late," she curtly replied. "I've already prayed for rain."

FOR WHAT DO YOU PRAY? How? To whom?

In far too many churches, the scenario unfolds like this: Someone says, "Let us pray." Heads bow, hands clasp, eyes close. Some immediately drop to their knees. For others the rule is to kneel with back erect when in prayer. No fair allowing the derriere to touch the pew unless you are sick, dizzy, retired, pregnant or wearing a leg brace.

The signs of a really *good* Christian are (1) callouses on the knees from praying, (2) the ability to kneel without holding onto anything for at least ten minutes or more, and (3) the capability of kneeling through the whole mass without flinching.

Many people don't pray unless they have a "ready made" prayer, or they use the Lord's Prayer for everything. They're scared to death to pray out loud, so inevitably they say, "Prayer is very private. I only do it in my bedroom or under my breath."

Then there's the content of the prayer. Many people see it as a sort of shopping list with variations on the theme. "Lord, here's what I need you to do." And then we state our list:

1. Find me a job; or help me find the job that is going to make a lot of money and be good for me (and quietly we mention salary, benefits, and driving distance to and from work).

2. Teach my spouse, boss, kids, or neighbors to be nicer to me.

3. Help me not to eat, smoke, drink, snort, or masturbate so much.

4. Take away my headache, heartache, stomachache, broken leg, or warts.

5. Make me taller, shorter, thinner, fatter (not uttered often), handsomer, or prettier.

Then there's plea-bargaining.

6. "Now, God, if you get me through this cancer, I'll go to church every Sunday for the rest of my life."

7. "If we win this court case, I'll give a big pledge/donation to the church."

8. "Make my wife more understanding about my affair, and I'll never use your name (or your kid's name) in vain again."

Then there's wheeling and dealing.

9. "Tell you what Lord. If you get me this big sale, I'll give you 7 percent."

10. "Get me this job and I'll never tell you a lie again."

Sometimes we get angry at the Benevolent Dictator.

11. "Why did you make me get sick?"

12. "How come you let that cop catch me?"

13. "You made me get a divorce."

14. "You gave us a child who is disabled."

15. "How come you let me get fired?"

We seem to make prayer so complex that most people are afraid to try. Those who are trained seem to do it so easily that we're convinced that only if one is ordained does one really know how to pray.

Is prayer that complex? I don't think so.

It's really only communication, talking, sharing. Prayer does not have to be said in King James' English in order to be understood. There is no right position. Bow your head or look up or straight ahead. Sit, kneel, lie down, prostrate yourself on the ground, lie in your bed, or sit in your car. You will have a listener.

For me, prayer is Creatively working out life's challenges. It is not "Get me a job," but rather "Allow me to use my creativity to go out in the job market well prepared to tell them who I am and what my gifts and strengths are."

It's "Give me the strength to be able to handle the rejection of 'No, we've hired someone else.' "

"Allow me to force myself to work at finding a (or keeping my) job on a daily basis."

"Help me to be aware so that I don't take out my frustrations on my family and friends."

"Don't let me blame everyone and everything else. I am responsible for myself. I have the freedom to pick and choose."

In Creative prayer, there is no shopping list, plea-bargaining, wheeling/dealing, "tell you what I need you to do." All that's useless. The Creator is not going to intervene, in spite of the fact that many Christians tell stories to the contrary. One of my favorites is my "born again" friend who went to one of the world's largest and busiest shopping centers at Christmas when it's very difficult to find a parking spot. My friend prayed to the Benevolent Dictator to find a spot—and sure enough, there was a parking spot close to the entrance. "A miracle." See? Prayer works. But the part he forgot to tell is that he drove around for about a half hour before the Lord found him the spot. A miracle? No, a pile of baloney.

Either we're born free or we're not. If we're not, why bother? If it's all planned and directed up there, why be responsible or Creative because it's really to no avail. So you might as well just stay in bed and let the Benevolent Dictator (or Master Puppeteer) take charge.

No, it's *not* that way. You and I are responsible for ourselves. Our prayers and communication need to reflect that. So keep them simple and down to earth, in everyday street language, responsible and creative.

Someone once said, "When we talk to God, it's prayer. When God talks to us, it's schizophrenia." (I think it was Will Rogers; if not, try Erma Bombeck.)

A form of prayer I often suggest to people who want to keep it simple is praying the cross, a method for private devotion employing the five forms of prayer in a logical order. When saying the prayer, look at a cross or imagine one. Or hold a cross in your hand and touch the five locations as you pray.

Say the words slowly. Do not rush. Make them your own. Add your own thoughts. Pause to fill in the blanks. Speak the names and needs of the people you pray for. Memorize the form. You can then say it anywhere and at anytime— walking, resting, wakening, jogging. If you find this helpful, share it with others.

There is a natural progression. Use it. It works, and as you will see, there is a reason for it.

The first thing we want to do is to recognize Creator/Creation. My wife and I live by the beach where we have beautiful sunrises and sunsets. What a way to start the day watching Creation create. It's awesome. By starting at the top of the Cross and acknowledging Creation we are immediately pulled away from ourselves and our perpetual "shopping list" of things that we want our Higher Power to do for us. In this first element, called "PRAISE" ①, we make such statements as "Glory to Creation, to Jesus my Christ, and to Creativity," or "Creator, I love you and all of your Creation," or simply "I love life." Just some short phrase that makes us look up.

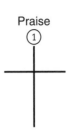

Now let's move to the left side of the Cross ② and give "THANKS" for things such as life: yours, mine, others', trees, birds, and even skunks (the animal ones as well as the human ones). Some of the other things I like to mention are my work, which I really enjoy; my ability to forgive; my capacity to love; my wife, whom I love very much and try to tell her so everyday; laughter; my ability to be sensitive to the needs of others. I always try to end this section with the idea "Help me to show my thanks in my living."

Next, I need to "CONFESS": admit to myself where I have "missed the mark" in my daily living. (Move over to the far right side of the Cross ③.) Perhaps in the last twenty-four hours I have thought some unkind things about others, I teased someone with a degree of viciousness, I insisted on having my own way, or my sexual fantasies veered off

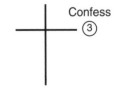

course. The basic idea is not to do this to make me feel lousy about myself, even though sometimes I need to. It does keep me in check and give me guidance and direction about the things that I need to do (love) and those things that I ought not to do because they feed into the power of the Destructive Force. Need to put it into more formal words? Try "Creator, I confess that I have separated and broken your law of love, especially by (name the ways and be honest) _____

_____

_____."

Now ask for forgiveness and move on with your life.

It's back to the center of the Cross ④ and my prayers/thoughts about "OTHERS." Maybe it's a friend who is terminally ill, a couple going through a divorce, a relative who has hurt you, a national disaster, your children, the boss, a homeless person, the myriads of fellow human beings whose lives seem so desperate and out of control. You may want to start this process with "Loving Jesus, who died for all, help and protect your children everywhere, especially _____" and go through your list. Remember, it's here at the heart of the cross that Jesus hung and died so that all humanity might live life to its fullest.

Others
—④—

Finally we are down to "SELF" ⑤. For me, going through the above exercise has narrowed my needs down to almost nothing. My own demands seem so petty in light of the hurting world around me that almost on a daily basis I simply ask for "more patience, understanding, and humility." On those days that I am facing some extra heavy challenges I will ask for the strength to utilize

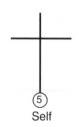

⑤
Self

my gifts and strengths to their maximum. Want more formality? Then "O Creator, love me. Grant me _____

_____ ."

Guide me in my work and play. Keep me brave, pure, and reverent. Help me to forget myself and think of others through Jesus my Christ and my Lord."

Very often I end by saying the Lord's Prayer.

This form of prayer is simple, straightforward, and easy to do on a daily basis. Prayer, or talking, communicating with Creator, has to be a part of our daily life. It keeps us honest with ourselves, the rest of the world and our Creator. Prayer is communication with a friend—a very close friend—I hope and one who accepts us as we are but challenges us to do more with our life.

CHAPTER II

Church versus church

A young woman, sitting in her chair, is watching television, with her boyfriend. "Bob, what a thrilling game. The congregation is going wild."

Her boyfriend, looking at her incredulously, says, "Don't you know that football games have fans and churches have congregations. Courtrooms have spectators, riots have mobs and accidents have onlookers.

The yound woman, still watching the game, replies, "The congregation just tore down the goalposts."

DOES YOUR CHURCH HAVE FANS? Or a congregation? Or an audience? Or spectators?

"church" and "Church" look alike and sound alike. Obviously, as one looks at the two words the only difference between them is a small *c* versus a capital *c*. But in reality, their differences are huge.

The church is a building, usually constructed in a particular shape, depending upon one's preferences. (Remember, there are over five hundred varieties of

Christianity.) Usually there is a person (called a minister, priest, clergyman, pastor, father, or reverend) in charge. Most of the time these in-charge persons have help (everyone wants to build their own kingdom here on earth). These folks come in the form of assistants, secretaries, sextons, yard people, business managers, choir directors, organists, paid choir members, soloists, full-time window washers, and so on. A rule of thumb: for many clergy, the more people in your kingdom, the more important you seem to be.

With all these people, all this property, all the furnishings, cars, and so forth, there usually needs to be someone in a higher position, so the little churches elect someone called a bishop, cardinal, monsignor, supervisor, executive director, executive secretary, or pope. Now that person needs a place to work complete with assistants. That takes money. Where do they get it? From the little churches. They pay a sort of franchising fee for the honor of running the little church on the corner.

Many churches also have national or international operations so they need an overall headquarters. This is called a different name, e.g., national headquarters, Vatican, home office, temple. It too has property, real estate, people, a building, and on and on and on.

The church is *big* business. It owns a great deal of real estate and property and has many people working for it. To be really honest, most churches are filthy rich. If you had their portfolio, I suspect that you would never have to work again. Of course, churches don't talk about wealth. They "poor-talk"; they never seem to have enough to pay their bills. Perhaps you could dig a little deeper so they can continue with their TV ministry, their cathedral, their choir. People must dig a little deeper because the radio and TV ministries must keep growing. The *big* business gets *bigger*. (And they pay next to no taxes to boot. How's that for a deal!)

New Christian schisms (breakaways) are happening all of the time because when people get mad, they start their own church. Remember Henry VIII? The Pope wouldn't grant him a divorce from his wife, so Henry started his own church. There are many people just like that today. Some people can't get their way, or they see the Bible from a different point of view, and another church starts. Some are thrown out of their own church and want to keep ministering. So they buy or rent a building and another schism is born.

How the churches love to bicker and name call. (I always want to say, "It would make Jesus roll over in his grave." But he's not in one.) Many of these churches are bigoted and prejudiced. They all deny it, but try to join if you are gay, divorced, mentally unstable, a different color, unkempt, a rabble-rouser, etc.

The churches love to argue over insignificant details. Many of these churches love to quote the Bible, usually out of context, to prove a point. (For example, "Wives must be submissive to their husbands." That's nice, except they forgot to read the rest of that chapter starting with Ephesians 5:21.[5])

They love to gain (and keep) control over their members. The churches insist members buy into the party line by telling them what to do, how to think, and what to say. They know how to make you feel guilty or poorly about yourself. Bad! Bad! God doesn't love you. God is the Benevolent Dictator or the Tyrant. He wants to hurt you, make you feel poorly about yourself, so you will be obedient. You are led to believe that the church is the keeper of the *truth*. It has the truth. It is the truth.

The church sells itself as sort of a cosmic comfort station. Come every Sunday. You have to go, regardless of how dull

---

5. Paul did say wives must be submissive to their husbands but with very specific guidelines: "(28) Even so husbands should love their wives as their own bodies . . . (33) However, let each one of you love his wife as himself."

the pastor, how awful the choir, how boring the service. Other times it feels like it's a three-ring circus at church. There are singers, dancers, special preachers, bands and quartets, special guests, and more.

Often the central theme of the church is for members to be "perfect." (See Appendix A, Obscene Words and Phrases.) Naturally, we can't do this, so the guilt and giving button is pushed.

I often wonder if Jesus could ever become a member of most Christian churches. After all, he's Jewish (and the church is primarily for Christians); he doesn't have any interest in the law (remember, he came to replace it); he wasn't baptized (or at least not like our baptisms today); he dressed funny (people would stare and feel uncomfortable); he never went to seminary (so obviously he couldn't consecrate the bread and wine the right way); and he hung around with a bad crowd (tax collectors, prostitutes, uneducated fishermen, and traitors).

I still believe that the church can and must be a part of our society. It has a very important role to play in being the training ground for Christians to prepare ourselves to go out into the real world and love our fellow human beings. Someone once said that the church has too much religion but too little faith. We can become too wrapped up in liturgy and forget that our worship is the tool that gives us the energy to leave the church to start loving what sometimes might be called the unlovable.

Now let's talk about the Church. It has no buildings. It is people—people with a common bond. Jesus is their Christ. They have made this commitment by being baptized in some fashion.

The Church is people who are alive and responsive to the Creativity around them. They understand their Destructive nature. They are not perfect and never will be. But they are forgiven and they know it. They have weaknesses and make mistakes. They know other people fail also, but that's okay. It's part of humanity and Creation.

They know they're born free. They make *every* choice in life. They know they can choose to be Destructive or Creative.

They know that they are responsible for themselves and no one else. Neither the Lord nor the Devil made them do it. Whatever they did in life, they did out of their own free will.

Christians are people who realize that their Christ saved them from the law. Jesus superseded all other laws with the law of love (originally set down in Deuteronomy and Leviticus by Moses).[6] This law of love is the only law that Christians have to obey. Man-made laws, or laws of the land, sometimes have to be disobeyed. Some of those laws are Destructive because they are so self-serving. Of course, one has to pay the consequences for disobeying the law; but sometimes one must do this in order to make sure that the law of love prevails (ask Martin Luther King or Bishop Desmond Tutu).

The law of love includes a lot of acceptance and forgiveness. It says "I'm sorry." It rights wrongs. It buries pride.

The members of the Church read the Bible and use it primarily as a guideline to live life by. They know that there are many other books as inspirational as the Bible, maybe even more so. A member of the Church never stops growing in "wisdom and stature and in favor with God and man" (Luke 12:52).

The Church can laugh at itself. The Church cares about people (regardless of their status). It constantly reaches out and ministers to the hurting world.

---

6. Deut. 6:5: "And you shall love the Lord your God with all your heart, and with all your soul and with all your might." Lev. 19:34: "And you shall love him as yourself."

It sees the church as a means—to bring people together to share—and not the end. The only end is to love, through all denominations, schisms, and heresies.

The Church supports and strengthens humanity of all sorts and conditions. This includes gays, divorcees, and prisoners. The members of the Church admit their hypocrisy. It reminds me of the bishop who was having dinner at the home of a woman who was greatly involved in the church. Her husband, however, never went. The dining conversation eventually turned to "church," and on and on the bishop and the woman talked. Finally, the husband could stand it no longer and interjected, "Bishop, do you know why I don't attend the church?" "No," replied the bishop. The man responded, "Because there are too many hypocrites." The bishop retorted, "Oh, that's okay. We can make room for one more." Hypocrisy is part of the human condition. The Church loves us anyway.

In my ministry, the entity that I feel is the closest to being like the Church is the organization Alcoholics Anonymous (or any of the Anonymous programs), a group of people who really support each other. To me, it seems to be Christianity at its purest. Unfortunately, or fortunately, it doesn't say a thing about Jesus as the Christ. Maybe that's okay because perhaps it's only through our freedom and our faith that you and I can say Jesus is my/our Christ.

When a church caught fire, the townspeople joined the volunteer firemen in fighting it. Throwing water right along with the rest of the bucket brigade was an old man who never attended any of the services there. The clergyman saw him and said, "This is the first time I've seen you at church." The old man replied, "This is the first time I've seen any fire in this church."

Is there any fire in your church? There's plenty in the Church.

LIVE CHURCHES, DEAD CHURCHES

LIVE churches always have parking problems;
dead churches don't.

LIVE churches have lots of noisy youth;
dead churches are fairly quiet.

LIVE churches are constantly short on staff;
dead churches usually have a surplus.

LIVE churches' expenses often exceed income;
dead churches always take in more than is spent.

LIVE churches grow so fast you forget names;
in dead churches everybody knows everybody's names.

LIVE churches support mission enthusiastically;
dead churches keep it all at home.

LIVE churches focus on people;
dead churches focus on problems.

LIVE churches are filled with tithers;
dead churches are filled with tippers.

LIVE churches dare to move out in faith;
dead churches operate totally on sight.

LIVE churches evangelize;
dead churches fossilize.

—Borrowed from someone a long time ago

CHAPTER 12

So Why Bother?

After the service the minister at the church door, said to a member of his congregation, "I'm sorry you're moving. You've been excellent sermon material!"

GENUINE CHRISTIANS, IN MY OPINION, are great sermon material. I love being a Christian. It adds a real dimension to my life.

I was born free and I keep on being free. I'm an individual and an individualist, and I must stay that way in spite of everyone trying to take my individuality away from me.

I was created by Creativity. (Remember God doesn't make junk.) I'm unique. There is no one else like me (that could be good or bad, I suppose).

I am important. No matter how minute I may seem to be in relationship to the universe, I'm still a very important part of Creation. As a result, I must love Creation and Creativity. Therefore, I must love myself (even when it's hard to do).

I have found a Christ. A Christ who has taught me how to be Creative. His name is Jesus.

The man was a very simple person with a very simple message: *love*. But it's not always simple to do. In light of Chapter 1 (Living in the Jungle) and Chapter 7 (The Bad News!), let's see how love relates.

Jesus said first of all we have to love ourselves. (If I don't or can't love me the rest doesn't make a lot of sense.) After we have learned to love ourselves, we then must love our neighbor and Creation. Here are some guidelines to help you do just that.

HOW TO LOVE OURSELVES
(the guidelines)

- *I am not talking about loving myself in a conceited way. Conceit is a form of insecurity and has nothing to do with loving oneself. I love me because I love Creation, and I am a creature of that Creation.*
- *I am Created to love.*
- *I love my strengths and gifts and also accept my weaknesses as part of my humanity.*
- *I am responsible for myself and cannot turn that responsibility for my life over to any other person or institution.*
- *I must be in control of myself and not allow anyone or anything to take away that control.*
- *I am born free (no strings attached), and life is a matter of making choices. I must continue to make them and pay the price for making a bad choice(s). Once a bad choice has been made, I must accept the consequences and move on—no fair wallowing in the past. That is not how I love myself. I can do nothing about the past. It's done and gone, but I can do something about the future.*
- *It's okay to make mistakes. It's a part of my humanity.*

HOW TO LOVE OURSELVES (con't)

Furthermore, no matter what I do I am forgiven just for the asking.

- *I am allowed to feel guilty—for maybe thirty seconds. Then I must move on. Guilt will kill me.*
- *I am allowed to dislike myself for a very short period of time, but during that process I must continue to love myself. (For example, I do not like me when I lose my temper, but I love me and my Creativity, which will help me keep my temper under control.)*
- *I must love and respect my uniqueness. There is no one else like me on earth—and maybe in the universe.*
- *I am the only "me" Creation created and it's my responsibility to get/keep "me" right.*
- *The "H" (hate) word cannot be in my vocabulary because it will kill me.*
- *I cannot become locked into self-pity. It serves no useful purpose and will only paralyze me. My pity pot went out with the trash a long time ago. Occasionally, I try to retrieve it, but I must throw it out again.*
- *I cannot be jealous. It's a blatant sign of my insecurity and will get me into a lot of trouble. Anyway, how can I ever be insecure when I know that in spite of myself, my Creator loves me unconditionally?*
- *I love my feelings. They are a temperature gauge of what is happening. Sometimes I don't like what I feel, but that's okay because my Creator gave me the Creativity to deal Creatively with all of my feelings— good and bad.*

*I MUST LOVE MYSELF so that I can
LOVE MY NEIGHBOR
(which includes every human being in Creation)*

- *This does not mean that I have to like every human being or have them like me. (That is humanly impossible. Even Jesus couldn't do that.) But it is humanly possible for us to "love" everyone.*

- *The "H" word is out. It will totally destroy me and them. It's one of the favorite tools of the Destructive Force.*

- *Conflict between myself and my neighbor is okay. It's part of my/our humanity, but I need to learn the law of love ASAP so that we can both move on with life.*

- *Forgiveness is the key to success in loving my neighbor. Not to forgive is to destroy me—probably before it destroys him or her. My ever-constant symbol is Jesus' willingness to immediately forgive those who crucified him.*

- *Acceptance is another key word and action. I have to accept people the way they are. I have to love (not necessarily like) the unlovable. My biases, prejudices, and bigotries have to go. They are tools of the Destructive Force. I must control them and not let them control me.*

- *I cannot control my neighbor's thinking or actions— and vice versa. She must make her own decisions about life and especially about such issues as abortion. I must respect her opinion but not let her push it on me when I disagree. I must agree to disagree.*

- *I must never let the sun go down on my anger. (This is a tough one because my pride gets in the way all the time. It's my worst enemy.)*

LOVE MYSELF

LOVE MY NEIGHBOR

LOVE CREATION

- *What a great feeling to know that I am loved unconditionally.*
- *I am forgiven just for the asking.*
- *I have been given the tools to lead life to the fullest— even though sometimes I either forget that I have them or forget to use them.*
- *I have been given more Creativity than I will ever use. But it's available whenever I want it.*
- *Sometimes it's difficult to believe that I have been born into total freedom. It's a great gift even though at times I abuse it. But I can't let anyone take it away from me.*
- *Death is a part of life, and I can't really live life to the fullest until I accept that fact and make it work for me.*
- *Fear is a part of life, and again Creativity has given me the tools to deal with it. I must use them.*
- *How could I not love Creation! This love is the key to making life successful.*

The Bad News is life can be awful. We are living in a jungle.

The Good News is love is the answer to living successfully in that jungle.

A very important aspect of being a Christian is to have the ability to understand my pride—to see it in its destructive nature and to see how it gets in my way, often stopping me from accepting, forgiving, loving.

I must develop an understanding of perfection (that there is no such thing). I can't be perfect and I don't want to be. And Creation does not expect me to be perfect.

My Christ teaches me about guilt. It's a great emotion—for thirty seconds. Don't hang on to it. It will make us sick—mentally, physically, emotionally. Allow it to warn us that something is wrong within our environment, deal with it, and get on with the rest of life.

He teaches us about anger—another tremendous emotion, the one we often abuse, misuse, or suppress. Let your anger flow, but let it flow Creatively. Deal with it on the surface. Talk about it like an intelligent human being, not a wild animal.

Jesus tells us what is destructive: hate; prejudice; bigotry; hostility; rage; selfishness; or being unforgiving/unforgiven, uncaring, indifferent, or negative. He also says the following *can* be Destructive: power, wealth, legalism, drugs, alcohol, institutional religion, obesity.

Where are we going to learn about all of these things that Jesus teaches us? First, in the church with the Church. Some of the world's most put-together people are in the church. Most of them are in the church because that's where they grow and nurture themselves, where they charge and recharge their batteries.

We're going to learn about all this in the Scriptures, which we must read daily. Because the Scriptures are so confusing, I recommend you read them with guidance, such as a study group or a publication such as "Bible Reading Fellowship."[7] The Scriptures possess guidelines, reminders, and eternal truths. But they also contain some fallacies that we must recognize and correct.

---

7. For more information, you can contact the Fellowship at P.O. Box M, Winter Park, Florida 32790.

Becoming a Christian is a quick and easy process through the simple act of baptism. Growing as a Christian is a lifetime process. It can, it must, never stop.

We're going to practice being a Christian in the church with the Church. But to really learn about our faith, we must take our Christianity out into the real world and use it with our fellow human beings. Not in the sense of pushing them into Christianity but showing them (through our actions) that within our lives, Jesus has made a difference in the way we act, talk, and relate. We can love them in spite of themselves.

There may be confusion at this point. Too often churches get into a numbers game. They are constantly evangelizing and pushing people to join. It is as if they get extra celestial brownie points if they can get people to become members. Not true!

There's a great story about a man coming home late from a party one night. Weaving and staggering, he tripped and fell into a deep, abandoned well in the middle of nowhere. He called for help, but no one came. He called all night and into the next day, but no one came. He was scared, so he started praying, "Lord, if you get me out of this, I'll give my life to your service." About dark, someone heard him and pulled him out. The man was eternally grateful. He joined the church and had a special ministry—going around pushing people into wells so that they would become Christians, just like he did. Unfortunately, there are too many well-pushers in the church today.

Next as Christians we're going to learn that in order to get the most out of our faith, we have to serve others. Jesus tells us over and over, "Whoever seeks to gain his life will lose it, but whoever loses his life will preserve it" (Luke 17:33). Mission, or outreach, is in our backyard as well as thousands of miles away. It's through mission work that we're going to grow the fastest and best as Christians. Because it's at that point we start to understand ourselves and realize the tremendous rewards in serving our fellow human beings.

I can remember the first time I discovered that lesson. I was fresh out of college, an officer in the Marine Corps. Usually at Christmas time, the group of people I ran around with spent a lot of time partying. That year, at Thanksgiving, we decided to do something for someone else rather than just spend our Christmas holidays figuring out where the next party was. We called the post office, which sent us a letter addressed to Santa Claus. It had come through the mail and was from a twelve-year-old girl who wanted to make sure that her four younger brothers and sisters received Christmas presents. Their father had tuberculosis and had to go into a sanitorium the day after Christmas. He could not work, and they were on welfare.

We shared the letter and checked out the story's authenticity. We made arrangements to be with the family on Christmas Eve after the midnight service. We had a marvelous time buying presents, food, and a Christmas tree. After the church service we piled everything into our cars and drove to a low-income housing area in south Philadelphia. The family was waiting. We had the most marvelous time sharing ourselves, our gifts, and each other with that family. In my own life, and in the lives of all of my friends, that particular incident was a turning point. We realized the great thrill and joy in sharing our lives with others. What a Christ Mass!

That reminds me of a great Christmas card we received from a young woman who was a hard-working volunteer in a deaf advocacy group we had started. It read: "Christmas presence—give yourself away." Think on that for a few minutes. It's the heart of the Good News.

Let's go back to my friend Sally whom we met in the Introduction. Remember she called me to discuss whether she should have her baby daughter baptized. Sally asked me some hard questions about Christianity and the church. I told her that I would write a book to answer her many questions. Well, I have written the book, but I'm not sure I have really answered Sally's questions about baptizing her daughter. So let me try now.

My immediate reaction is don't bother at this time. As suggested earlier, nothing magical is going to happen to her daughter at her baptism, and in no way do I see her daughter being excluded from a life after this one because she wasn't baptized.

What I feel is more important at this time is for Sally and her husband to examine their relationship with a Higher Power. Do they see Christianity (after having read this book) as something that they would like as a part of their lives, or at least would like to examine more closely? If their answer is no then why bother having their daughter baptized? She is not going to be raised in an atmosphere that will nurture her growth in the Church or as a Christian. It is sort of like buying a beautiful new car and then parking it in a garage. If you don't take it out and use it, it's not very useful.

If Sally and her husband decide that they would like to deepen their relationship with Creation, then I would suggest that they sit down together and discuss the kinds of things they think they want in a church, i.e., preaching, teaching, type of worship (formal or informal), outreach to the hurting world, their stance on hot-button issues (abortion, gays, women, etc.), cost of joining, their individual and collective expectations, and whatever else might be important.

Now it's time to go church shopping. Talk with friends, neighbors, relatives, co-workers. Do they attend a church?

Have them describe their church. Match what they tell you against your list. Select one or two churches to try. Make plans to attend, at least a week in advance, with the solemn vow that nothing short of death is going to stop you from going. (It is amazing how many excuses one can find on Saturday evening and early Sunday morning *not* to go.) Try the church of your choice at least two or three times. Once you return from church, discuss the pluses and minuses of that church. Remember, there is no such thing as perfect, and the perfect church does not exist.

Church shopping is very much like car shopping. The chance of finding the right church for you on the first try is about as remote as finding the right car at the first dealership at which you stop. Shopping could take as long as six months, but finding the right church will be worth it. Once you find the church that feels most comfortable, become involved. Attend church, go to classes, and start to say prayers at meal time, before you go to bed, and when you get up in the morning. Read your Bible on a daily basis; become involved in outreach to the hurting world. With all this happening, now is the time to discuss baptism—for adults and children.

I think that maybe I can hear Sally and her husband saying, "Wow, that's a lot of work!" I agree, but I think you will find that having the faith that Jesus is your Christ will add a dimension to your life that is almost indescribable. I follow a daily Bible reading study (called "Bible Reading Fellowship") and found this thought after the Sunday, January 19, 1992, reading (John 4:14).

> After I had made a serious and specific commitment of my life to God, there was a change in the way that I experienced the people and familiar sights and sounds around me. There was a sense of newness. It was like smelling the moist earth after a spring rain. I enjoyed the

ordinary things of life more—like tasting food and seeing sunsets. And I was engulfed with a wave of gratitude because I felt as if I were a child who'd found out he was "loved by the teacher."

This says it for me, and it's the truth.

Sally, in your quest for a church in which you can grow as a Christian, and in which you can be the Church, let me suggest a guideline that I call Bad News/Good News. A Bad News church will try to take control of your life and tell you how to think, has lots of laws or rules, labels people, centers their teachings on the Bible rather than on Jesus and love, thinks their way is the only way, puts church before Church, gives token offerings to the hurting world. A Good News church is talking a lot about love, is accepting of people the way they are, and is going out into the real world, loving every speck of it.

After having read the book and knowing Sally very well, I suspect she would probably ask, "Can I really get to heaven without going to church?" Yes, Sally, of course you can because heaven isn't a place. Rather "heaven" is a loving relationship with ourselves, our fellow human beings, and Creation. And if Jesus is your Christ, he is going to give you the tools to be a "lover" and allow you to experience that sense of newness that will make you think that you are in heaven.

Postscript

I HOPE YOU HAVE ENJOYED THIS BOOK or at least it has made you think.

The book says many things in a very short space. Much of it is new and provocative and maybe even a little threatening.

A suggestion: After your first reading, wait a few days or a week or two (at the most) and then try it again. I think you will see that many of the ideas and thoughts presented here will fall into place. You will even see things the second time around that you missed the first time. Maybe you will even laugh a little harder at some of the jokes.

Above all, I hope that you will discuss it with your friends and family because that's why it was written—to make people think and talk about their faith.

"Obscene" Words and Phrases

WARNING! Please do not read this appendix if (1) you take the institutional church too seriously, (2) you can't laugh—especially at yourself and the world around you, or (3) you make your living from selling "church" (sometimes called evangelizing).

There are certain words that we banter around that cause a lot of problems. They confuse our thinking. Some of them mess up our whole lives. This is how I look at these words, but within the context of this book I am going to try to avoid them. Inevitably, they only confuse the issues.

"C and E" FOLK: Christmas and Easter folk. The "alumni" return on those great days to collect their warm fuzzies and maybe some "celestial brownie points."

CHRISTMAS: An afterthought. Three and one-half centuries after Christ's death, Emperor Constantine thought it was a good idea to counteract a drunken Roman festival. It worked for awhile. Now we've come full circle and the merchants love it.

FORGIVE AND FORGET: Sort of a Christian saying. The first part is okay. But unless you have an IQ of 25 or a bad case of amnesia, the second is impossible. So forget forgetting.

GOLDEN RULE: "Do unto others . . . ." Sounds good but not very practical. God loves us—in spite of ourselves. No, Jesus didn't advocate the Golden Rule. He was for love. Try it His way.

GOD: A cross between Santa Claus, a Master Puppeteer, and a Benevolent Dictator. (See chapter 3.)

GOD'S WILL: It's usually something bad that makes us hurt or feel miserable about ourselves. Or it accounts for drunk drivers causing accidents and babies being born with handicaps.

GOOD WORKS: Something most Christians think they have to do in order to go to heaven. Clergy jump on the band-wagon because it gets people to church. Fortunately, we are saved by our faith so there's no need to collect any celestial brownie points.

HEAVEN: Up there. Only good guys get to go. Are you going?

HELL: Down there. Fire. Horned (horny?) men running around in red costumes with tails and pitchforks. It helped Dante sell a lot of books. It is not a place. It's a relationship—or lack thereof.

HOLY SPIRIT: A ghost. Whispers in good guys' ears in the middle of the night. Most Christians really have no idea about what or who he is so they rattle off theological jargon about who they think the Holy Spirit (or Ghost) is.

HERESY: Whatever you believe and I don't. To substantiate his/her belief, the sayer (with little or no background of the religious history of that writing) usually quotes a marvelous Biblical passage out of context.

JUDGMENT: Something we like to do to each other—trying to figure out who will make it into the Kingdom and who won't. Something we know that God does to us all day long.

MIRACLES: I sure wish Jesus hadn't performed any. He has confused people down through the centuries who tend to see him as a first-century Houdini performing a whale of a magic show. Good Friday and Easter have become secondary.

PERFECT (Perfection): There is no such thing. Except in the eyes of the beholder. A great many people strive for it but never make it. They can't. Many Christians think that is what Jesus wants us to be. Also, most people think that Jesus was perfect. But they never asked his parents, Judas, Pontius Pilate, the religious leaders of the day, or the pig farmer who lost his herd when Jesus put a demon in them. (See Luke 8:32.)

PRAYER: Little talks with God, usually telling him (or her) what to do. Must be said in the right position: kneeling (on hard concrete), head bowed, eyes closed tight (no peeking), crossing oneself at least three times per prayer, uttering either Latin or Elizabethan English.

PRIDE: The dirtiest word in the English language. (See chapter 7.)

PURGATORY: A cop-out. A figment of someone's imagination. Of course, it's better to go there than "down there," and since only a few good guys go up, the rest of us have to go someplace.

REVEREND: A title used (mostly misused) for a religious person who has received orders. It's really an adjective that should always be preceded by "the," i.e., the

Reverend John Deer or the Reverend Mr. Deer or the Reverend Mrs. Doe.

SACERDOTALISM[8]: One of those long theological words that means *only* the Rev (see above) can perform a holy act such as baptism, confirmation, consecration, unction, and so on. (It's really only a job guarantee.) If true, sacerdotalism would have eliminated Jesus and the Twelve from doing any of the sacraments. After all, they did not go to seminary and had no degrees.

SEX: Dirty. Christians don't talk about it or even think about it. Jesus never had it. Mary and Joseph didn't do it. It's too bad some Christians feel negatively about it. It's really a lot of fun.

SIN: Whatever seems to be fun or fattening. Some churches have long, long lists categorizing sins under "bad," "really bad," or "really, really bad."

SINNERS: Fat people who have a lot of fun. Or everyone but me. Or no one but me. Or people who have too much fun. You name it.

SOUL: One of those words that means nothing. Have you seen one? Where is it? Most Christians talk about the immortality of the soul. Sounds good, but it has nothing to do with Christianity. That heathen concept goes back to Greek mythology.

SPIRITUAL: Another one of those theological words that sounds good but means nothing. Implication: holy. One looks, acts, or smells holy by saying and doing the right thing. It often involves lots of scraping, bowing, crossing oneself, wearing a five-pound crucifix on a heavy metal chain around one's neck, and/or hurling around heavy theological words.

---

8. Sacerdotal—of priests, priestly. Sacerdotalism—the system, spirit, or methods of the priesthood. Usually disparaging.

TURN MY LIFE OVER TO THE LORD: A cop-out phrase. Meaningless, but sounds good to "spiritual people." The Lord (whoever that is) doesn't want your life. It was given to you and you are responsible for it, to live in complete freedom and to pick and choose. I knew a lady who "turned her life over to the Lord." After her second divorce, she took it back and started being responsible for it. Things have been better ever since.

TEN COMMANDMENTS: A list of laws established by Moses (who really plagiarized them from the Egyptians, who stole them from the Babylonians, who borrowed them from the Neanderthals). Most Old Testament Christians love them (because they love the law). Jesus threw them out in favor of the Law of Love.

VIRGIN BIRTH: What a mess that story created. It was easy for Greeks and Romans to buy into it because of their heavy belief in mythology. But that doesn't mean that intelligent people should believe it. Please note that Mark and John avoided it like the plague.

WRATH OF GOD: Earthquakes, tornadoes, hurricanes, volcanoes, etc. Drunk drivers. People's handicaps. (See God's Will.) Most Christians imagine God as an angry old man whose main mission is to make everybody, especially believers, miserable.

The following space is for you to use to add your own list of obscene words and phrases used by spirituals:

_____

_____

_____

_____

_____

Saved by Faith

READ THESE PASSAGES. It will only take you a few minutes. When you finish, there should be a tremendous sense of relief. Now you can get to heaven without even going to church. (The emphasis in the following passages is mine.)

1. *Romans 3:20–31:*

For no human being will be justified in his sight by works of the law, since through the law comes knowledge of sin.

But now the righteousness of God has been manifested apart from law, although the law and the prophets bear witness to it, the righteousness of God through faith in Jesus Christ for all who believe. For there is no distinction; since all have sinned and fall short of the glory of God, they are *justified by his grace* as a gift, through the redemption which is in Christ Jesus, whom God put forward as an expiation by his blood, to be received by faith. This was to show God's righteousness, because in his divine forbearance he had passed over former sins; it was to prove at the present time that he himself is righteous and that *he justifies him who has faith in Jesus.*

Then what becomes of our boasting? It is excluded. On what principle? On the principle of works? No, but on the principle of faith.

For we hold that *a man is justified by faith* apart from works of law.

Or is God the God of Jews only? Is he not the God of Gentiles also? Yes, of Gentiles also, since God is one; and he will justify the circumcised on the ground of their faith and the uncircumcised through their faith.

2. *Romans 5:1–11:*

Therefore, since we are *justified by faith we can have peace with God* through our Lord Jesus Christ. . . . While we were yet helpless, at the *right time* Christ died for the ungodly. Why [we] will hardly die for a righteous man. . . . But God shows his love for us in that *while we were yet sinners Christ died for us.* Since, therefore, we are now justified by his blood, much more shall we be saved by him from the wrath of God. . . . We shall be saved from his life. . . . We rejoice in God through our Lord Jesus Christ, through whom *we have now received our reconciliation.*

3. *Romans 6:1–11:*

What shall we then say? Are we to continue in sin that grace may abound? By no means. How can we who died to sin still live in it? Do you not know that all of us who have been baptized into Christ Jesus were baptized into his death? "We were buried therefore with him by baptism into death, so that as Christ was raised from the dead by the glory of the Father, we too might walk in newness of life."

For if we have been united with him in a death like his, we shall certainly be united with him in a resurrection like his. "We know that our old self was crucified with him so that the sinful body might be destroyed, and we might no longer be enslaved to sin." For he who has died is freed from sin. But if we have died with Christ, we believe that we shall also live with him. For we know that Christ being raised from the dead will never die again: death no longer has dominion over him. The death he died he died to sin, once for all, but the life he lives he lives to God. So *you also must consider yourselves dead to sin and alive to God in Christ Jesus.*

4. *Romans 10:4:*

For Christ is the end of the law, that *everyone who has faith may be justified.*

5. *Galatians 2:15–17:*

We ourselves, who are Jews by birth and not Gentile sinners, yet who know that *a man is not justified by works of the law but through faith in Jesus Christ,* even we have believed in Christ Jesus, in order to be *justified by faith* in Christ, and not by works of the law because by works of the law shall no one be justified.

6. *Galatians 3:23–28:*

Now before faith came, we were confined under the law, kept under restraint until faith should be revealed. So that the law was our custodian until Christ came, that we might be *justified by faith.* But now that faith has come we are no longer under a custodian; for in Christ Jesus you are all sons of God, through faith. For as many of you as were baptized into Christ have put on Christ.

7. *Ephesians 2:8–9:*

For *by grace you have been saved* through faith; and this is not your own doing, it is the gift of God—not because of works, lest any man should boast.

8. *Titus 3:4–8b:*

But when the goodness and loving kindness of God our Savior appeared, he saved us, not because of deeds done by us in righteousness, but in virtue of his own mercy, by the washing of regeneration and renewal in the Holy Spirit which he poured out upon us richly through Jesus Christ our Savior, so that *we might be justified by his grace* and become heirs in hope of eternal life. The saying is sure.

9. *Hebrews 2:9:*

But we see Jesus, who for a little while was made lower than the angels, crowned with glory and honor because of the suffering of death, so that by the grace of God he might taste death for every one.

Perhaps you have some passages that you would like to add:

_____

_____

_____

_____

_____